Praise for *The Celti*

"*The Celtic Way of Seeing* inspires and equips all of us, regardless of our personal heritage, to perceive the world around us with wiser and more compassionate eyes. By breathing new, visionary life into the ancient myths and rituals of the Celts, Frank MacEowen helps us map a better future for ourselves and for humankind."

— Jack Maguire, author of *Essential Buddhism, Waking Up: A Week in a Zen Monastery*, and *The Power of Personal Storytelling*

"*The Celtic Way of Seeing* is an important contribution to the reclaiming of indigenous wisdom for modern life. Frank MacEowen's deep insights into what he calls the Irish Spirit Wheel places it alongside the medicine wheels, mandalas, and sand paintings of other Earth-honoring cultures. I heartily recommend this book for everyone wanting to deepen their connections to the vast horizon of Celtic spirituality."

— Tom Cowan, author of *Yearning for the Wind*

Praise for *The Mist-Filled Path*

"The power of personal experience to enlighten, guide, and activate resonates undeniably throughout Frank MacEowen's *The Mist-Filled Path*. Peer within these pages into the mists of your own connection to our world and the divine. May this book guide you into heartfelt conscious action on behalf of all that is sacred."

— Julia Butterfly Hill, activist and author of *The Legacy of Luna*

"A rich and poetic book that seems to bring together the very best aspects of the Celtic vision of the world. Warm, personal, and adventurous, this is a book that should be read by everyone remotely interested in the human spirit."

— John and Caitlín Matthews, authors of *The Encyclopedia of Celtic Wisdom*

"*The Mist-Filled Path* reads like a memoir but with a call to action on every page."

— *New Times*

"A distinctive and evocative book that makes a worthy contribution to our understanding of Celtic tradition and, best of all, inspires us to participate in Celtic consciousness."

— R. J. Stewart, author of *The Merlin Tarot*

"*The Mist-Filled Path* is a beautiful and passionate description of a soul journey along the old Celtic roads between earth and sky. It is also a spirited invitation to collective soul recovery, inviting us to reclaim ways of being and seeing that were shared by our ancestors.... This book is a gift and a delight."

— Robert Moss, author of *Conscious Dreaming*, *Dreamgates*, and *Dreaming True*

"Frank MacEowen is an astute learner, a visionary teacher, and a sensual storyteller.... An illuminating and important work. I recommend it highly!"

— Oscar Miro-Quesada, Peruvian kamasqa curandero and founder of the Heart of the Healer Foundation

PRAISE FOR *THE SPIRAL OF MEMORY AND BELONGING*

"Frank MacEowen is one of the very few permitted to get a glimpse into the realm of the shining ones by ancestral guardian spirits of Ireland."

— Martin Duffy, director of the Irish Centre for Shamanic Studies

"For those who are exploring Celtic mysticism or shamanic spirituality, Frank MacEowen's *The Spiral of Memory and Belonging* is an imaginative map of one wanderer's journey through the kaleidoscopic realms of nonordinary states and personal mysteries."

— Bill Plotkin, author of *Soulcraft: Crossing into the Mysteries of Nature and Psyche*

THE
CELTIC WAY
OF SEEING

OTHER BOOKS BY FRANK MACEOWEN

The Mist-Filled Path
The Spiral of Memory and Belonging

THE CELTIC WAY OF SEEING

MEDITATIONS ON THE Irish Spirit Wheel

FRANK MacEowen

New World Library
Novato, California

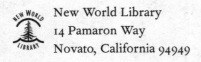

New World Library
14 Pamaron Way
Novato, California 94949

Copyright © 2007 by Frank MacEowen

Text design and typography by Tona Pearce Myers

Library of Congress Cataloging-in-Publication Data
MacEowen, Frank.
  The Celtic way of seeing : meditations on the Irish spirit wheel / Frank MacEowen.
      p.   cm.
Includes bibliographical references (p. 127) and index.
ISBN 978-1-57731-541-4 (pbk. : alk. paper)
  1. Celts—Religion—Miscellanea. 2. Wheels—Religious aspects—Miscellanea. 3. Spiritual life. I. Title.
BL900.M443 2007
299'.161446—dc22   2006038280

First printing, March 2007
ISBN-10: 1-57731-541-3
ISBN-13: 978-1-57731-541-4
Printed in Canada on 100% postconsumer-waste recycled paper

g New World Library is a proud member of the Green Press Initiative.

10 9 8 7 6 5 4 3 2

This book is lovingly dedicated to my biological parents and to those many individuals who have served as spiritual parents to me as well. You know who you are.

A wheel was shown to me,
wonderful to behold…
Divinity is in its omniscience and
omnipotence
like a wheel,
a circle,
a whole,
that can neither be understood,
nor divided,
nor begun nor ended.

— HILDEGARD OF BINGEN

contents

FOREWORD

HORIZONS

I t's really about the sun. And the moon and stars. This constant rising and setting, the slipping of day into night and back again. The turning of tides, and time, and seasons. The ambiguous line we call the horizon plays a crucial role in helping us know who we are, where we are, and where we are going. The sun, moon, stars, and planets rise in the east, cross the sky, and disappear in the west in their endless circuit of eternal renewal. Something in that progression is supremely satisfying to the human soul. Something says to us that we too are part of this great rising, crossing, and setting. And return.

The horizon might be as old as the soul itself — or even older — and as enduring. And, like the soul, it always lures us further into our own lives and into the great mystery of Life Itself. The horizon is an edge, a spirit edge. It does and does not exist. Or, more accurately, it does not exist in ordinary reality, for we can never reach it or touch it or stand there. Horizons keep moving away, challenging us to go further. The line where sea and sky or hill and cloud meet is in some sense imaginary, yet we can see it. It does not exist, and yet it is so real that we cannot live without it. It is part of the landscape that we must know — and also imagine — if we are to live to our fullest potential.

Both the soul and the horizon are imaginal; that is, they are made up of images, constant presences that surround us, embrace us, move through us. We know they are there, those images, but often we are not aware of them. Or, seeing them, we fail to grasp their importance in shaping our lives.

If we are here for "Soul-making," as John Keats tells us,[1] then we must bring the images of our souls to life, bring them up over the soul's own horizon into view. In doing so, we build up that wisdom for which the soul longs. Like stars waiting with their new light to rise over the eastern hill, our life experiences wait to be noticed, examined, reflected upon, and made conscious. Thus our experiences turn into wisdom. We fill the cauldrons of our souls with wisdom of the infinite — infinite because it comes from beyond the horizon.

Life and soul unfold within the horizon. We are always standing in the center of our lives, and in the great center of Life Itself. As the earth spreads out from us in all directions, our souls naturally unfold and expand to meet it. As the horizon keeps hurrying off beyond our journeys to it, our souls naturally explore and search further into the mystery of the world. The retreating horizon can fill us with awe.

We suffer without the horizon. Is solitary confinement in prison the worst conceivable punishment partly because it robs a person of that necessary horizon? Does working in a windowless room do the very antithesis of what it is intended to do, namely, protect the worker from distractions? Living without a horizon is one of the greatest distractions. It cramps the imagination; it stifles the soul's need for wildness, for adventure, or simply for free breathing.

Indigenous people live consciously with the horizon. Along that great rim of the world they discover places of spirit and power. They acknowledge the four directions that square the circle. For them, these are places where human life can find both the material and spiritual sustenance it requires.

The circle with a cross drawn through it is one of the oldest symbols found around the world in Paleolithic rock art. It is a universal symbol of something sacred. There is something very satisfying about this image, for the circle is an unbroken line, without sides or angles, each point on its circumference equidistant from the center. It seems perfect. And into this circle of perfection there are four equal pathways, from the top and bottom and from the two sides. These four entries into the circle meet at the exact center. If we lay this image on the earth, we recognize the horizon and the four directions that encompass us. We can see that this sacred symbol can stand for the sacred space in which we live, or hope to live. Indigenous people consciously make the places where they live sacred, with prayers, blessings, virtues, meanings, and dreams that bring those four cardinal points of power alive for them.

If you love gazing out to the horizon, you will love this

book. It will make the four directions come alive for you. In it, Frank MacEowen retells one of the most intriguing stories of ancient Ireland, a story in which we discover how the early Irish people viewed the horizon and the spirit places along its rim. Then he calls us to go out there with him, onto those placeless places along that rim and discover the mysterious way in which that old Irish horizon encompasses our entire lives. Here you will find courage, wisdom, music, gift giving, laughter, work, persistence, conflict, love, and longing. You'll find your whole life here. And you will discover the Celtic way of seeing your life, as you stand in the center of it, look outward and onward, and wonder.

— Tom Cowan, author of *Yearning for the Wind*

intRODUCtion

One of the images that appears on the screen of my laptop computer is a rotating aerial photograph taken in Ireland. The photo is of an expanse of the Boyne River Valley, which is named for the Irish goddess Boann. The photo includes a bird's-eye view of the famous Hill of Tara and looks toward the south, the province traditionally known as Munster. I keep the photo in my line of sight, daily, to remind myself of some of the principles in this book and to consciously call to mind one of the sacred sites of my ancestors — a site currently endangered by the forces of modernity and by so-called development.

I gaze at the photo and take in the scene, much as I do when I stand there in person, looking out at the rolling wood-lined hills, the patchwork of fields, and the horizon line of the Boyne Valley. I take a breath, close my eyes, and I am there, turning to face the East, the South, the West, and the North.

It was from the Hill of Tara — at different points in history — that the island of Ireland was ruled, first by the Dananns (also known as the Tuatha Dé Danann, perceived as a pantheon of gods by some and considered an ancient race of humans who preceded the Irish Celts by others), and then, later, by the *Ard Righ* (ard'rah), or High Kings of the Irish Gael, the incoming Celts who seized the country from the Dananns.

The selection of this site by whatever peoples originally constructed it in the ancient past was not an accident. From the vantage point of the Hill of Tara one can see out to the horizon in all directions; it is one of the perennial high points in the Irish landscape. Tara's importance, however, is not limited to the practical role it played historically.

Though the Celtic world is filled with abandoned hill forts used as villages and military fortifications, equally as prevalent in Celtic lands are various mountains, cairns, hills, and sparsely wooded mounds that have long been associated with spiritual observances, ritual, and places for seeking vision. Tara happens to be both — the site of an ancient hill fort and also a place that has repeatedly been used for pilgrimage, communion with the land, and conscious spiritual orientation by practitioners within the traditions. In Celtic and Irish spirituality, places like Tara are holy. They are sites of pilgrimage and meditation. When we go to places like Tara we touch, albeit briefly, what happened in the past, and we *touch in* with living energies in and around the place that anchor us both spiritually and culturally.

Many people who visit the Hill of Tara — even for the first time — report feeling various sensations and emotions. People receive "impressions" and "flashes of memory," similar to what happens at other "power places" around the world. Tara is one of those classic *thin places*, as described in Celtic tradition, energetically alive with history, with the imprint and presence of things that went before. But it is equally alive with all manner of spiritual associations invisible to the untrained eye or to the soul that has not yet been initiated into the *mouth-to-ear transmission* that is a vital function of Celtic storytelling tradition.

Tara's obvious horizon line also brings it alive. Such horizon lines are numinous in Celtic spirituality; they represent a Celtic way of seeing. These lines are the reason many Celtic people have always traditionally sought high hills, mountain peaks, and forested mounds for places of prayer and vision seeking. Such places can grant us a vaster perspective than we are habitually accustomed to, not only in the literal sense as we stand in a high place looking out over the landscape, but also in the personal sense as our spiritual vision of our *inner world* and outer life expands.

The power of the horizon line takes on added meaning in Ireland, and most especially at Tara, where each of the cardinal directions is imbued with a set of deeper and not always obvious "teachings." We might think of these teachings as one of the tributaries of embedded spiritual *gnosis* (knowledge) in the Celtic tradition.

The four *airts* (an Irish and Scots Gaelic word meaning both "winds" and "directions") are connected to spiritual patterns and influences of great significance to the tradition and the life of the practitioner. Though this way of seeing is uniquely Irish, the influences themselves are universal. If you are open to them, these spiritual energies, associations, or teachings (however you prefer to think of them) will grant you access to the wisdom of very ancient patterns of experience and insight, regardless of your background. As you invoke these creative wisdom energies and bring their energy to bear on your life, you will find yourself becoming more conscious of your passage, more enriched with inspiration, stronger, bolder on your path, and more grateful for your life.

Although one *could* relate to this four-directional template simply as a way of appreciating the ancient lore of Ireland, with her different regions, qualities, and cultural expressions, from the perspective of the ancient Irish mystery traditions, this approach would merely be skimming the surface. If we look at this ancient knowledge as a way of orienting to the deeper energy of our lives and as a kind of meditative map, then it becomes a spiritual tool that can facilitate awareness, bravery, and growth.

Because of their relevance to universal subjects, the associated meanings and influences of the Irish Four Directions (as well as the axis mundi, which is often referred to in mythology as the archetypal center of the world) represent an ancient way of being, a Celtic way of seeing, a way of orienting to life's energy, and a way of relating to the various experiences, lessons, and challenges that emerge on the soul's journey.

This spiritual map is a *mandala* — an ancient Sanskrit term meaning "circle" and often referring to circular designs that portray balance, symmetry, and completion. Mandalas appear in almost every culture. These symbolic circles, which can be seen in everything from esoteric Buddhist iconography to the *mesas* (or sacred altars) of certain practitioners of Peruvian shamanism, can serve as sacred reminders of the path we seek to walk, connecting us with deeper teachings. Sacred Hindu *yatras* (mandalas specifically used for meditation), stained-glass mandalas in Chartres Cathedral in France or Glastonbury in England, the Native American medicine wheel, the yin yang symbol from the ancient Chinese tradition known as Taoism, and the "solar cross" or "Celtic cross" from the Celtic-Christian tradition: all are examples of mandalas.

Probably one of the greatest spokespeople for the power of mandalas was the Swiss psychologist and consciousness explorer C. G. Jung. For Jung, mandalas were external representations of the unconscious and of one's psychological integration. Jung believed that when we meditate on mandalas, and when we draw and paint them, they open us up to different levels of spiritual reflection and inner work.

The same is true of the Irish mandala presented in this book, which I will refer to as the *Irish Spirit Wheel*. As you read you will come to see that this circular image symbolizes different aspects of the human soul as well as different levels of experience on the spiritual journey, that they provide a way to engage with the more deeply embedded teachings and spiritual energies to which the primal Irish tradition is oriented. These teachings and energies, although ancient, are quite relevant to our lives today, for the themes and challenges of the human journey through life are perennial. As you engage and interact with this ancient mandala, you are encouraged, each step of the way, to return to a core question: *How does my life journey relate to the journey of the wheel?*

Whether you do in-depth ritual work or engage in simpler, subtler, but no less powerful ways of holding you and your life issues in the heart of this circle, if you journey deeply with the content of this book — consciously and intentionally — you will find parts of yourself stirring awake. As this occurs, you will hear a calling. Spiritual influences, energies, and insights that are part of the primal Irish tradition, that are waiting to come to your aid, will beckon and invite you into a deeper relationship with your life.

In essence, once you know the orientations of this ancient Irish mandala and understand the living energies associated with each direction, you will find infinite ways to apply the wheel to your life. As you move through these pages, you will be taken on a brief contemplative journey where — in addition to unveiling some of the deeper aspects of the Irish directional perspective — you will, I hope, slowly find yourself "walking the wheel of spirit," learning to relate both to the deeper challenges and to the everyday features of your life in a new and vital way that is, at the same time, part of an ancient tradition.

A WORD ABOUT THE CELTIC WAY OF SEEING

Before we proceed, I would like to say a bit more about what I mean when I use the term *Celtic way of seeing*. By *seeing*, I do not mean with the eyes exclusively. A partially or completely blind individual still has the capacity to see in the Celtic way; we all do. In this book you are essentially being invited to explore an intuitive way of seeing, a spiritual way of seeing, a way of seeing in which the heart, the inner reaches of the mind and soul, even the body, are transformed into a set of "eyes."

I am also not implying that this book contains a description of every nuance, angle, or expression of the Celtic way of seeing. The book you are holding can only serve as an invitation to a deeper part of you that already knows. In fact, one could remove the word *Celtic* altogether and substitute whatever term speaks most to you. At the end, perhaps you will call this way of seeing something completely different, for example, the "Zen way of seeing," the "ecopsychological way of seeing," or the "way of seeing with the awakened heart."

Indeed, these expanded ways of seeing are not limited to the Celtic traditions. On the contrary, among the Japanese and Lakota, for instance, we find specific cultural terms that speak equally well to this kind of seeing. In Japan, the word *dairokkan* (die'ro'ken) means "intuition" and translates literally as the "great eye," while in the Northern Plains traditions of the Lakota the idea of the *cante ista* (chan'tay' ish'tah), or "eye of the heart," is a central teaching of some of the medicine people.

An example from the Celtic world appears in the Scottish Highlands, where we find the term *da-shealladh* (daa'halugh), which translates as the "two sights," denoting the capacity to see both the normal waking world (ordinary reality) and the world of spirit and energy that is inextricably connected to this one. The two sights, as a spiritual way of seeing, is expressed throughout the Celtic world — ancient and present — among certain individuals, such as the *bruadaraiche* (broo'a'tar'a'kar: "dream-seer") and the *taibhsear* (tah'shar: "vision-seer").

A kind of mystique surrounds seers in every culture, and yet many of them will tell us that what they do is nothing special; they just pay attention to what most people ignore. As practitioners, we can all apply ourselves to discerning subtle patterns of the "waking dream" by relaxing the normal constraints of everyday thinking, tapping into a flow of intuitive information and wisdom, one type of which Jung referred to as *synchronicity*. The Irish Spirit Wheel is but one way of kindling these capacities within us. If we awake in the morning, face each of the directions, consider the lessons that each direction holds for us, and actively bring our life issues to the sacred wisdom inherent in this Irish mandala, we will find great strength, immense relief, and deep insight each day.

Those who have gotten away from the "eye of the heart" and the "great eye" of their intuition may consider the ways of seeing described in this book as fantastical, otherworldly, or supernatural. Yet these ways of attuning to the deeper spiritual knowledge are commonsense perceptions in what I call *energy-sensitive* cultures, which include the Taoists of China, the Huichol and Mazatec Indians of Mexico, the Q'ero of the Andes, and and the Sami Lapplanders of Finland. The original Druids, too, are examples of such cultures. They were learned men and women among the Celtic tribes who served as wisdom keepers and seers, offering these deeper perceptions to their culture.

These and other cultures maintained a dynamically heightened connection to the earth and the spiritual phenomenon of lucid wakeful dreaming. They knew — and have always known since — that these subtle ways of perception can connect us deeper to life and to the powers of the Otherworld, an invisible realm of energy, wisdom, and healing power that is perceived and expressed in different ways in different cultures.

Dear friends of mine who are initiates in the ways of the

Andean Q'ero suggest that the Q'ero are so profoundly energy sensitive that they are able to identify and remove diseases from the bioenergetic field of a person *before* an ailment, cyst, or tumor has a chance to manifest in the dense reality of the cells of the body. When asked how they do this, my friend and Peruvian shaman Oscar Miro-Quesada replied, "The Q'ero live more in the spiritual world than in the physical one. Their spiritual eyes are particularly attuned to discern subtle energies that the rest of us in the industrialized world — with our atrophied senses — can hardly imagine."

While there is no one approach to spiritual seeing or intuiting, it is fair to say that most seers have been shaped by an intentionally slower rhythm (such as that found in meditation), that they have been formed by spiritual traditions stressing multidimensional realities (within and outside the self), and that they often take retreats or choose to live in quiet rural settings.

In her *Ravens & Black Rain*, Elizabeth Sutherland states:

> Through strictly observed rituals they [Celtic seers] were taught to tap their latent psychic powers, so that they might enter a collective dream state where natural and supernatural realms merged in a timeless dimension. Celtic mysteries occurred in twi-states between night and day, in a dew that was neither rain nor river, in mistletoe that was neither plant nor tree, in a trance state that was neither sleep nor waking. The Christian sense of duality — good and bad, right and wrong, black and white, body and soul — was unknown to the druid. The key to Celtic philosophy is the merging of dark and light, natural and supernatural, conscious and unconscious.[1]

It is in this spirit of embracing a slower and more intentional rhythm, of embracing the dark and the light, the natural and "supernatural," the conscious and the unconscious, that we will explore the Irish Spirit Wheel.

HOW THE BOOK IS ORGANIZED

The first part of *The Celtic Way of Seeing* provides an overall orientation to myth as a living spiritual force, just as relevant today as it was in ancient times. In chapter 1, we will explore the spiritual nature of the Celtic storytelling tradition, as well as one of the pivotal concepts with which the druidic and bardic tradition works: *mythic memory*. As you work with the Irish Spirit Wheel — and as the "spirit of the wheel" sets itself up in your heart and awareness — you will find mythic memory and the deeper intuitive aspects of this Celtic way of seeing stirring within you.

In chapter 2, we will encounter one of the wild, wandering spirits of Irish tradition — an old shaman-poet named Fintan. Through a brief modern retelling of a much longer Irish story known as "The Settling of the Manor of Tara," we will learn about Fintan, the wider trajectory of his many spirited lives, his encounters with a unique spiritual being who possessed great knowledge, and how the ancient mandala and four-directional model came into existence.

These are among some of the oldest surviving Celtic spiritual cosmologies — sacred orientations that have been handed down to us from druid-poets via the bardic oral tradition, as well as through the later written record of Irish myth cycles. The various versions of this ancient Irish story survive today owing to

Celtic Christian monks who recorded the story from still-living lore keepers of their era.

However, in recording the tale — a story believed to predate the coming of the Church to Ireland — these monks took certain liberties with the story, adding aspects of their own tradition and worldview to the more ancient Irish beliefs. For our purposes, I have attempted to return to the essence and spirit of the story by omitting any overtly Christian representations, leaving for us a more streamlined view of the wheel, wherein lies the doorway to the teachings. For those who feel a particular affiliation with versions of the story that bear the mark of a monk's pen, no offense is intended. I merely desire to make the story and the deeper teachings of the wheel accessible to a wider audience who may be from a variety of other traditions, or no tradition at all.

In chapter 3, we will explore certain aspects of the Irish directions as a form of sacred mapping, not only of the Irish landscape, but also of the inner soulscape of the human being. I, of course, do not believe the Celtic tradition, or the Irish Spirit Wheel, to be the only path of growth and awareness; indeed, as a seeker and spiritual practitioner I glean just as much from the life philosophy and practice of Aikido and Japanese Buddhism as I do from the ancient spiritual view of my Irish ancestors. Nonetheless, I feel there are some particularly crucial aspects of the structure and orientations of this "glowing wheel" from the Irish tradition that can offer us a vital perspective on how to lead a life of balance and healthy power.

In that spirit, in chapter 3, you will find an elaboration on the traditional or core themes and associations of the Irish directions (as transmitted to us from the ancient story), as well as some insights into a contemplative way of relating to these orientations. Having learned of the associations of the mandala from the story in chapter 2, in this section we will begin to dance with a more expanded sense of the Irish Spirit Wheel, slowly coming to comprehend how these orientations can support us and direct us to what will enrich us, strengthen us, and aid us in our life journeys.

In part 2, we will begin our actual journey through and around the wheel with a series of reflections and thematic meditations. We will begin in the Center position of this ancient mandala in chapter 4, move to the East in chapter 5, to the South in chapter 6, to the West in chapter 7, and to the North in chapter 8. Each reflection is followed by short meditations, reflection questions, or exercises designed to serve as places of pilgrimage and points of contemplation throughout your turning days and nights.

In this time of chaos, disconnection, discord, and destruction in our world, may this book — in some small way — assist us in finding the sacred horizons of our life again.

PART I

THE CELTIC WAY OF SEEING

ORIENTING TO THE SPIRIT OF THE WHEEL

I

MYTHIC MEMORY AND REMEMBERING THE FUTURE

The mythic present is continually reshaping events, whereas history
alone merely chronicles the tides of time. History deprived of its
mythic context becomes petrified into sound bites of the timeline;
but when myth inspirits history, we hear the voices of the past with
our own ears, see the images with our own eyes.

— CAITLIN MATTHEWS

The Celtic traditions are deeply rooted in the power of myth and memory. Indeed, for many Celts — homeland, postdiaspora, urban, and rural alike — myth and memory are inextricably intertwined. This truth does not have to translate into blind or naive literalism for those who practice the traditions deeply. It does mean, however, that at every turn a symbolic quest or important spiritual lesson awaits us when we give ourselves over to the Celtic spiritual vision.

Mythic memory is like a muscle. Exercised, it can become a vital gateway of perception, inspiration, healing, and spiritual connection. Yet it can also become atrophied. When this occurs — as it has in the modern world — it takes dedication, practice, and focus to recover the élan vital of mythic memory. When we do, we regain the sacred senses and way of seeing of the ancestors.

To reconnect with the spiritual guidance of the mythic past — what we might think of as "mythic memory rehabilitation" — we must enter into the heart of the myths themselves to feel, once again, their sacred pulse, thereby also awakening something in the ancient blood coursing through our veins.

Whether or not you are Irish, whether or not you are of Celtic descent, when you encounter, in the next chapter, the core story that inspires this book, I invite you to read it a few times. Read it once as you would read anything. Then read it again and see if you can *visualize* more deeply in your mind's eye the events depicted in the story, even placing yourself somewhere within the tale, perhaps as someone standing there observing. Finally, practicing the Celtic way of seeing, soak in the story again and allow your *heart* to open to its mystery, and see if you gain any deeper sensations or insight about the tale.

Mythic memory is an invisible thread that stitches those of us in the present day to the "deep time" of the ancestors — whatever our ancestry or ancestries may be. A myth, or a mythic story, is not just a quaint tale or a form of entertainment (though many Celtic stories can be quite entertaining!). A myth as sacred story is a gift from the past providing an empowered path into the future for us to journey along. Exercising mythic memory stokes a very ancient and intuitive way of knowing — a potent, symbolic, and integrative way of seeing that was known to all our ancestors.

Sacred story can speak to us of timeless lessons (many of them painfully relevant to us in our present age) and offer us different ways of looking at our innermost being. In this way, the mythic past (which we can encounter through mythic memory) is not "dead and gone" but is, rather, a living energy, a functional reference point, what Celtic spiritual teacher Caitlín Matthews refers to as the "mythic present."

From ancient songs and epic poems to accounts of battles and various wonder tales, the Celtic traditions have always emphasized spiritual continuity. Celtic spirituality, in addition to being a path of honoring nature, is an enduring process of orienting to the invisible thread of memory as a means of enriching life. This spiritual dispensation still exists, as evidenced by lore that has been passed down for thousands of years, as well as by the variety of ongoing innovations that clearly reflect a thriving Celtic spirit today.

An Irish friend of mine put it most succinctly when he said, "We are still here," a sentiment shared by another friend from Celtic Wales, who shares her sentiment that "the ancestors live through us. Their stories are our stories. Their way of seeing can be our way of seeing." With the story you will encounter in the next chapter, as well as with any myths or tales you investigate from other cultures, the task becomes to "enter" the story, to make it your own, to have it live and breathe through and within you.

Indeed, it is precisely because of the power of story that we have a surviving Celtic tradition at all. Story is stitched to memory. Story is woven to breath. Story is laced within blood and bone. Story pulses within dream and vision. In Ireland, Scotland, Wales, England, Brittany, the Isle of Man, Cornwall, and innumerable postdiaspora Celtic enclaves around the world, even today one can hear the still-vibrant stories of brave chieftains and warrior-poets, great feasts and battles, druids and warrior queens, Otherworld voyages and encounters with various spiritual beings.

Despite this living thread of Celtic storytelling, at times the stories, wisdom, sacred knowledge, and intent of the traditions have been misplaced or seemingly forgotten, leading to a state of mythic crisis. When we become disconnected from the mythic roots of who we are, this often translates into a loss of our spiritual way of seeing and being.

In the Irish epic known as *The Tain* (*The Tain Bo Cuailgne*, or Battle Raid of Cooley), for example, we learn that all the great poets and storytellers of Ireland were once called together in a council by the Chief Poet of the island. All the lore keepers were summoned, because it was discovered that a particular story of a famous cattle raid was no longer intact. Different poets knew different sections of the tale, but none of them knew the full story. The Chief Poet of Ireland — known as an *ollamh* (o'lav) — hoped that by gathering all the most learned bards of the island they could piece back together the ancient story. They could not.

The full story was not fully recollected until a young poet named Muirgen sat down at the graveside of a once great poet named Fergus Mac Roich. After offering a small praise poem in honor of the ancient bard, Muirgen suddenly found himself enveloped in a mist. Standing before him, deep inside the mist, was none other than the spirit of Fergus Mac Roich. For three days and nights, Mac Roich transmitted *The Tain* in its entirety to the young poet. I guess we could say this was the first meeting of the "Dead Poet's Society."

Though no one knows for sure why we "forget" sacred knowledge of the past or how we lose our connection to a spiritual way of seeing and living, it is clear that we have done just that. Perhaps knowledge and wisdom slip away because we take for granted those things in which we are or were deeply steeped; as Irish poet John O'Donohue suggests, we can become so familiar with something that we cease to truly see it. And as we cease to see something we gradually forget it. Songs, stories, lore, customs, and sacred orientations — all these can fade from memory, and when they do we must recollect them to reestablish the proper order of things.

The following abbreviated story from ancient Ireland portrays the forgetfulness that can lead to a state of mythic crisis. Hailing from the time of Diarmid mac Cerball (545–565), this tale — known in its more voluminous version as "The Settling of the Manor of Tara" — portrays a time of confusion and disagreement, when some of the nobles of Ireland had to turn to the mythic memory of an old lore keeper to regain an important part of the Irish tradition: the sacred orientations of the island itself.

2

THE KNOWLEDGE IS
IN THE DIRECTIONS

An Abbreviated Telling of
"The Settling of the Manor of Tara"

H ave you ever lost your car keys? Better yet, have you ever
been on your way to somewhere familiar, suddenly realizing — that for one reason or another — you have become
lost? Perhaps you keep something in a particular place in your
home and have grown accustomed to finding that object there
whenever you need it. And yet one day you suddenly forget
where you have put it.

Even a tiny detail, such as a forgotten email password, can
throw life into chaos. We forget our phone number, an important
date (hopefully not our wedding anniversary!), a banking PIN, or
the name of someone we know and have bumped into in a setting

that is out of context. We can't remember the combination to a lock. We forgot an important meeting with a client. The particular order of facts and information that we rely on to maintain balance has become temporarily inaccessible; that is, *until something comes to our aid and reminds us.*

In the following story, the characters have become forgetful of certain important principles that ensure a harmonious relationship with other human beings and with the land. As they comprehend their forgetfulness, fear takes over, and suddenly they find themselves caught up in conflict. Some characters are ruled by an unchecked ego, a greedy energy that worries only about itself. For others, chaos and tension ensue. As a collective they find that they must invoke a holder of wisdom, one whose mythic memory and insight can guide them back to understanding and balance.

A voice rumbled from deep within the hall.

"Where are the nobles?" one of the High King's advisors snapped, at no one in particular. "It is the custom that they and their retinue attend the Great Feast! They should be here by now."

A druid standing nearby nodded in agreement. "Indeed, you are correct. They are not only expected to be in attendance, they are expected to contribute to the feast itself, as it has always been done."

The two men looked at one another and knew something

was amiss. They had felt a disturbance in the Great Peace for quite some time and had noticed the seeds of chaos beginning to sprout. The usual harmony of the land and of their souls had gradually entered a troubled state.

It had always been the custom for the nobles of Ireland from the far reaches of the island — lesser kings and chieftains alike — to travel every three years to the Great Hall at Tara: to sit in council, to swear fealty to the High King, to attend a banquet in his honor, and then to aid in giving a grand feast to the Irish people over several days of celebration.

It was an ancient observance, an ancient feast that involved music, storytelling, foot races, horse races, jousting, as well as the announcement of marriages, all against a backdrop of ale drinking and lovers courting. The Great Feast was a way to honor the bounty of the land, to recommit the bond between the High King and the land, and to maintain the memory of who they were.

Custom also dictated that the nobles and chieftains visiting Tara bestow various gifts from their respective regions as a gesture of homage to the king, including honey, milk, cattle, game, fine cloths, berries, nuts, newly fashioned weapons, even gold. Likewise, the nobles from the different regions of Ireland were expected to offer a portion of goods, food, and mead to augment the Great Feast at Tara.

This year was different. The nobles had traveled to the Hill of Tara. They had gathered. Yet they had not entered the king's fortress, or the Great Hall. Instead they stood with each other discussing a troubling matter.

"I do not understand why Diarmid, son of Cerball, has taken such a large measure of land for himself," one chieftain announced.

"What? Are you daft? He is the *Ard Righ*, he is your High King," another chieftain barked. "It is within his right to occupy Tara and her surrounding lands."

A noble from the southern hills cleared his throat and spoke. "As we all know, High Kings are married to the land. When all is right in the land, the land, in turn, provides for the people. The well-being of the people is dependent on the well-being of the land. The well-being of the land is dependent on the proper order of things. Maintaining the proper order of things is the responsibility of us all, king, druid, and commoner alike. With that said, I can find no fault with this king. And yet I find that I have lost the knowledge of the proper order of things, within and without. I feel as if a fog has settled on my brain. Where is the common spirit to which we all order our lives?"

A chieftain from the northwest argued, "I still do not see what this king needs with such large tracts of land for the manor of Tara, but I too must confess, now that we are discussing it, and knowing that the arrangement of the land must follow the proper order of things, I am ignorant of the great harmony that has ordered the inner and outer worlds from the Before-Time to This-Time."

After much discussion, the chieftains and nobles realized they were divided on the matter of whether the Great Feast should proceed according to plan.

Finally, an elder announced, "I do not share your concerns about the king, but I am disturbed that none of us can call to memory the sacred configuration of the island, the intended arrangement of Tara, or the intended alignment of things within each of our souls. I know enough to know that they all must be aligned with each other. With that said, I suggest we postpone the Great Feast until we can determine — once again — how to see the proper order of things."

With that, the nobles and chieftains decided to send someone up to the main gates of the Great Hall at Tara to convey their message. A sentry stood guard at the gate and intercepted the messenger.

"The nobles of Ireland have a message for the High King. They are not in full agreement regarding the matter, but they have decided that they cannot attend the Great Feast this year until that particular matter is settled."

"And what matter might that be?" the sentry asked.

"Some of the nobles feel the *Ard Righ* has taken far more than the king's portion of land. Others of us are uncertain but know full well that the arrangement of Tara, just as the arrangement of things within us and within our home provinces, must be guided by the proper order of things. However, none of us possesses the knowledge of this proper order, and thus we are uncertain about whether the king has taken more than his due for the manor of Tara. Until the manor of Tara is settled, partitioned, and resolved, and until we can discern — once again — the sacred alignment with which we all must live in accordance, the nobles are forced to boycott the feast."

The sentry raised an eyebrow. He knew the manor of Tara had always had the same defining boundaries as it did now — at least within his memory.

"Very well," he replied sternly and turned on his heel, moving quickly into the main compound at Tara. He passed through a shadow cast on the ground by one of the ramparts, giving the illusion that he had disappeared into thin air.

†HE PROPER ORDER OF †HIΠGS: A REFLECTIOΠ

Imagine living in a society that had been oriented to a particular code, ethic, or set of principles that ordered the flow of life — both internally, forming each person's spirituality, and externally, governing the people and the lands. Then imagine that, rather suddenly, for one reason or another, no one could recall what those governing principles were and thus they were unable to invoke them.

This is the difficulty at hand in this ancient story. At first glance, we might assume that the story is antiquated and thus irrelevant to our times. However, how would you experience the story if you were to reread the previous section and each time

you encountered the words the *proper order of things* you replaced them with other words, such as *democracy, civil liberties,
civil rights,* or *human rights?*

We are also living in a time — collectively — when some of
the more enlightened principles of our common humanity, the
basic and assumed "proper order of things," are being ignored
or forgotten. We must slow down and invoke the deep insight of
mythic memory so that we can return our lives, families, communities, nations, and the global village to a state of harmony.

As we return to our story, you will see that the nobles and
the High King do just that — they invoke the guiding memory
of one who can return all to a state of harmony.

After several moments, four sentries returned, accompanied by one of the spokesmen for Diarmid mac Cerball, the
High King.

"The king has heard your dispute. However, he does
not feel that what you ask of him is fair. He knows of no
ancient custom for dividing or partitioning the manor of
Tara beyond the current arrangement. He does not feel that
he can make a ruling on this matter without consulting the
lore keepers."

An older man with a graying beard spoke up in the group
of chieftains and nobles: "We concur that consultations are
required in this matter, for therein lies our disagreement.
None of us knows what the proper order of things is meant

to be. We implore the king to call forth those who hold this knowledge. Until this matter is settled, we cannot attend the feast."

Many days passed, valuable days that could have been used preparing for the festivities. A number of learned men from various parts of Ireland were summoned to give counsel about the proper order of things, yet each time the summoned party would make the same remark: "I am not the one to rule in this matter. There is a far wiser one than I."

In time, one of the individuals summoned to Tara announced to both the High King and the assembled chieftains and nobles, "There is only one man to whom you can turn in this matter. He is very old, very wise, and he knows the original sacred alignment that governed both the soul of the land and the souls of her people. Without that knowledge you cannot hope to resolve either the matter of the manor of Tara or the lack of harmony within each of you. The land and the soul are linked. You must seek out Fintan the Wise, a seer, a poet, and a hermit who has lived through many ages, and in many shapes."

When Fintan arrived at the assembly, the chieftains bowed at the regal sight of the old man. Young poets who had gathered to watch and record the historic event trembled, for they had heard all the days of their lives how Fintan was the wisest man on the island. The nobles each paid homage to Fintan, bowing as he passed them.

One of the chieftains whose lands bordered the High

King's, and who seemed particularly vested in having the matter addressed, suggested that Fintan take his place in the judge's seat. The old forest hermit pounded his staff on the floor and admonished the noble with a voice like thunder, surprising a great many in the hall with the strength of his utterance, coming as it did from the body of such an old man.

"I will not sit until I have heard all sides and exactly why I have been asked to offer judgment!"

A spokesman for the High King announced, "There is both a dispute here, O Wise Fintan, as well as a matter of grave concern to each of us. Some of the nobles here have challenged the High King. They feel that the current boundaries of the manor of Tara are too great. Additionally, knowing that such things are arranged based on the ancient knowledge and that similar principles of alignment exist for human life, we have all discovered — even our druids — that we are without such knowledge."

A druid added, "Wise Fintan, elder to us all, none among us holds this knowledge. We do not know the proper partitioning of Ireland, the arrangement of Tara, or the nature of the holy directions that envelop us. It is as if our minds are engulfed in a mist."

The nobles, some of them seeking more land and riches for their smaller kingdoms, chimed in, "We believe the current measure of Tara is too excessive. Upon what are the current measurements based? We are told that you can speak to such things."

Fintan gazed at the floor for a moment, then slowly made his way to the judge's seat. Before sitting, he looked into the eyes of the High King, reading his intent, discerning all the things that dwelled in the man's soul. He nodded, knowingly.

Then Fintan scanned the faces of the nobles. Most of them were earnest, but a few of them shuffled uncomfortably, for it had been said that Fintan had the eyes of a hawk and could read a person with but a glance. Fintan sat down and fell silent, searching his mind and his memory. After several moments of silence, he spoke.

"Ireland was my mother long before she became a kingdom of men, long before her glens and valleys were filled with paltry nobles squabbling over land. I was suckled at her breast, made wise in her many shades of knowledge, renewed in life and death in the waters of the Boann, and laid to rest one thousand times over in her caves, streams, bogs, lochs, and nests on high. When I speak today, I speak for her, and for all that I have seen and been."

The hall fell silent. All in attendance leaned closer in anticipation of what the old man might say.

"I am Fintan, son of Bochru. I have been a one-eyed salmon. I have been an eagle. I have been a hawk upon the wind. I have been a man of verse. I know of every people who have ever occupied this green land. I have survived flames and spears, swords and great floods. I dined with Parthalon from the East, hunted with Nemed from the North, and lived among the Fir Bolg of the Darkwood. I lived for a time, in-a-time-that-had-no-time, among the Tuatha Dé at Sliabh Anerin, and I lived in the tragic time when the Sons of Míl arrived and bore arms against them. I have seen the rising and falling of kings like waves on the sea."

"Clearly your memory is great," one of the bards from a noble's court declared. "What can you tell us of Tara, what can you tell us of the partitioning of Ireland, what can you tell us of the spirit behind all these things, what can you tell us of how you came to hold such knowledge?"

Fintan sensed the doubt that some had felt on his arrival was beginning to leave the room.

"So many questions, and yet these things are easy to relate," Fintan replied. "For this is not the first time I have sat here in an assembly at Tara, and it is not the first time I have been interviewed about the proper order of things, within and without."

Fintan took a deep draught of mead, then scratched at his beard. He began to relate a story to the assembled nobles and druids; it was a story that dripped with magic and age.

"A long, long time ago, at another gathering — much like this one, in the reign of Conaing Bececlach — a mysterious being, a spirit-man, was seen coming from the West at sunset. He was like a man, but he was not a man as we know men today. When this spirit-man reached the area of the assembly, sentries of the High King at that time were sent forth to invite the stranger to join the gathering."

Some of the bards looked at one another, recognizing something of this ancient story. They knew they had heard some shred of it before, but because of its great age it had passed from common telling.

Fintan continued.

"The spirit-man, taller than a tree is tall, asked those gathered at the assembly what they wanted with him. They informed him that they wanted to know where he had come from, where he was going, and what his name was. He said his name was Trefuilngid Tre-eochair, a keeper of knowledge, and that he was traveling from the Land of the Setting Sun to the Land of the Great Eastern Sun."

"And what came of this mysterious path crossing?" another bard asked Fintan.

"The spirit-man asked those assembled if any of them knew the chronicles of the ancient hearth of Tara, how the land should be divided, and if any were present who could relate to him the proper order of things." Fintan explained. "But the poets and druids informed the spirit-man that none among them could relate all the accounts, nor could they tell him the original law, the sacred order within and without that would ensure harmony."

"So this has happened before, Wise Fintan?" the High King asked.

"Aye, it has," Fintan responded. "As I've said, I have seen the rising and falling of kings like waves upon the sea."

Everyone fell silent for a time. A dreaming dog twitched

at the feet of Diarmid mac Cerball, the High King. A fire crackled in the center of the room. The wind could be heard blowing outside.

Fintan continued.

"It was at that time that Trefuilngid Tre-eochair announced, 'Bring together in council here all the most learned poets from every quarter of Ireland. I will then impart to you the sacred teachings of a wheel in whose spirit you will live. From this spirit you will work toward inner and outer harmony, arranging the land and the Hill of Tara accordingly. The wheel will become the center of your life.' With that, runners were sent to gather poets and seers from every part of Ireland. It was at that time that I was summoned to the assembly to hear the words of the spirit-man."

"And what did the stranger impart about Tara, about the spirits that govern this land, about the partitioning of Ireland?" one of the nobles asked.

"It is easy to relate, for his voice was wondrous like birdsong, his knowledge vast like the gleaming sky at high sun," Fintan replied. "And it was me — the oldest seer and poet of the island — to whom he entrusted his knowledge. But, like all knowledge worth knowing, it did not come until he had tested my memory as a container worthy of holding it."

"And how did this come about, great one?" Diarmid mac Cerball inquired.

Fintan's face lit up with a smile, betraying that a part of

his soul had traveled back in memory to the encounter with Trefuilngid Tre-eochair, and that he was speaking to the gathering of nobles from that place.

"It was none other than the spirit-man himself who tested my mind, questioned me, interrogated me, tested the mettle of my memory," Fintan explained. "He said to me, 'O Fintan, worthy of sight and verse, how is it that Ireland in all her beauty should be arranged, and what are the guiding spirits of each direction that can guide people in their lives?' I replied in earnest, for I knew: 'Knowledge dwells in the West, it is where we soak in wisdom; battle dwells in the North, the only true battle being the one within, it is where we go to test ourselves, to challenge ourselves, to refine ourselves; prosperity dwells in the East, it is where we learn of the bounty of life and how to share it; music dwells in the South, the place where we heal our senses and remember the Great Song; and sovereignty dwells in the Center, where we are in right standing with our destiny, the people around us, and the earth beneath us, as it always has been, as it will be from now until the end of time.'"

"And what did the spirit-man say to that?" a young bard asked, hanging off the edge of a wooden bench.

"He responded with affirmation, of course," Fintan said with a laugh, razzing the curious poet.

The hall filled with laughter.

Fintan took another draught of mead, and became silent again for several moments, for he was not merely relating historical facts. Fintan was reminding yet another generation of the sacred principles of the great Irish Spirit Wheel that would guide them in their lives as poets, musicians, druids, leaders, warriors, artisans, and seekers of wisdom; without the teachings of the wheel that encourage living in alignment with the proper order of things, he knew he would have to come back again and again to remind them of the sacred law. He looked into the eyes of the High King, and scanned the faces of the gathered nobles and chieftains before continuing.

"The spirit-man replied to my pronouncement, 'Thou art surely excellent in the craft of memory, Fintan. Each of the directions has her knowledge and a power waiting there that can teach us, guide us, temper us, and heal us. Her knowledge of learning and vision, her stories and histories, her understanding of the Otherworld, her counsel and beauty, dwell in the West; her knowledge of battle and warriorship, rough places, tempering and boldness, pride, hardihood, and conflict, dwells in the North; her knowledge of prosperity, of householders and householding, of hospitality, of abundance and gratitude, dwells in the East; her knowledge of music and inspiration, of poetic art and fate, of melody and advocacy, of waterfalls and life force, dwells in the South; her knowledge of sovereignty and enlightened warriorship, of dignity, primacy, and mastery, of stability and destiny, high kingship, and principality, dwells in the Center.' And with his description of Mother Ireland's knowledge and the dwelling places as such, I knew I was truly in the presence of a great being who had surely received all the knowledge and wisdom of this land."

When Fintan finished retelling the ancient story, a peaceful calm settled over everyone present. The nobles looked at their High King with new eyes of understanding. They knew he was fit to be their leader. The High King looked at the nobles with new eyes of compassion. He knew that all of them, himself included, had been under the sway of a profound forgetfulness. With the account of the mysterious spirit-man, of the living wisdom of the wheel, and of the sacred knowledge of Mother Ireland in each of the directions, something long cherished and vital had been restored in all of them. They remembered who they were. Everyone looked at Fintan. In that moment they realized even more fully the true power of the Celtic storyteller, one who heals the world with words.

3

SACRED DIRECTIONS,
LIFE DIRECTIONS

Do not forget to pay your respect to the four directions each day.

— MORIHEI UESHIBA, FOUNDER OF AIKIDO

In the story recounted in the last chapter, "The Settling of the Manor of Tara," we are taught an ancient map. We learn that West is associated with knowledge, North with battle, East with prosperity, South with music, and Center with sovereignty. In this chapter I would like to delve more deeply into the associations of the different directions to give you an even more tangible sense of how these energies are perceived in the primal Irish tradition.

These simple associations can be misleading if we take them

too literally. For example, Dublin (in Irish, *Dubh Linn*, or Black Pool) — originally a Viking trading post and now a thriving epicenter of international commerce, trade, and technological development — is one expression of Irish prosperity. Yet just because Dublin is in eastern Ireland, that does not mean it is the only example of prosperity in all Ireland.

Along the same lines, certainly Northern Ireland — also known as Ulster — has been host to sectarian violence stemming from the British occupation and the ongoing conflict surrounding Orangemen marches and unfair representation in government, but are we to assume that all conflicts have been limited to the North simply because "the Troubles," as they are known, exist in this part of the island?

Although these are compelling examples of specific locations and events expressing some of the themes of the four *airts*, we should not let our view of the directions become too narrow; Irish history and culture tell us that there have been multiple expressions of battle, prosperity, music, and knowledge in every part of the island. Seeking such hard-and-fast applications of the directional associations causes us to overlook something very important: the *inner* teachings connected to the four *airts* and the Center. By relaxing our habitual need to seek concrete interpretations, we can surrender to the more intuitive process of contemplative living and poetic seeing engendered by the Celtic spirit.

This process is hinted at by the spirit-man when he suggests to Fintan that each of the directions possesses various tiers of meaning, association, power, and gnosis. (My brief telling of the tale included only a partial list of the associations from the original story.) Trefuilngid Tre-eochair — the mysterious visitor who comes to Ireland, encounters the initial gathering, and shares his knowledge with Fintan — shares that in the West one will find learning, vision, stories, histories, counsel, beauty; in the North, battle, warriorship, rough places, tempering, boldness, pride, hardiness; in the East, prosperity, abundance, hospitality, householding; in the South, music, inspiration, poetic art, fate, melody, advocacy, waterfalls, wisdom; and in the Center, sovereignty, enlightened warriorship, dignity, primacy, mastery, destiny, stability, high-kingship, principality. We will discuss the deeper energies of the wheel in more detail below.

Taking into account these layers of images and associations, including how they are held together in an integrated mandalic whole, it becomes easy to see why the primal Irish view of the four *airts* (and the Center) is not just a map of an island but also of the human being, a map of the soul-in-process, and — when we consciously journey through the teachings of the wheel — a path of experience and gradually deepening insight that unveils itself to us.

By establishing a conscious practice of consulting each of the directions, in time we find that a storehouse of energy connected to the wheel becomes accessible to us. *Our life becomes the wheel*; the wheel becomes a living, interactive energy symbolizing different aspects of our psyche, our soul. When we spend time with the deeper aspects of the wheel, we are cultivating the deeper aspects of ourselves.

This Irish mandala is a sacred way of seeing, an ongoing journey — moment to moment, day by day, and over a lifetime — of awareness, mythic memory, inspired living, and inner tempering. It also embodies *enlightened warriorship*, a term used in the Shambhala teachings of the late Tibetan lama–warrior-poet, Chögyam Trungpa, who coined the concept to refer to the universal expressions of disciplined bravery. The Shambhala teachings are a concentrated body of ancient lore that Trungpa achieved access to and articulated in contemporary language.[1]

An important emphasis of the Celtic tradition — and therefore of this book — is on working with the Irish Spirit Wheel from more than just an intellectual point of view. Whether we are referring to the tempering energies of "battle" found in the North or the process of seeking vision and knowledge in the West, these aspects do not remain quarantined to the conceptual domain; they are integrated into the body, worked with within the psyche, even explored within the Dreamtime — that domain of nonordinary experience often accessed through dreams, meditation, or shamanic journeys.

In the Celtic way of seeing, a direct link between the eye and the heart is made, and this linkage can connect us to powers, energies, and knowledge that exist beyond us. Indeed, those Irish people who work with the wheel shamanistically (that is, who enter into nonordinary states of consciousness to connect with wisdom and healing energy of invisible realities) often perceive the different directions as spirits, guides, and protectors; for them, the spirits of the four *airts* are tangible presences, and dwelling at the very center of the wheel is the Goddess (more on Her in chapter 4). But whether we use it as a shamanic process of communication, a contemplative path, or a tool of transpersonal psychology, the Irish Spirit Wheel helps us wake up to our true nature.

Let us now turn to fuller discussion of these deeper teachings and reflections of the Irish Spirit Wheel.

JOURNEYING THE IRISH SPIRIT WHEEL

One of the central teachings of the Irish mandala has something in common with the teachings of any other mandala one might find across cultures; it concerns cultivating a life of awareness and balance.

The different qualities of a mandala represent different qualities within us — our highest, most enlightened expressions, as well as those parts of us that need transformation and refinement. This process of transformation and refinement is what enlightened warriorship is all about, and any good mandala represents the full spectrum of who we are and contains the steps to take us toward realizing all the points of that spectrum.

The Irish Spirit Wheel teaches us the lessons of healthy power, as opposed to the kind of imbalanced power that haphazardly destroys life. It teaches us a conscious practice of maintaining the sacred harmony of life — the physical, spiritual, and psychological life of the individual as well as the health and harmony of the community and the land on which the community is dependent. For our purposes here, by *community* I am referring to both human and nonhuman relatives.

Though it is rarely discussed in pop-Celtic literature, the traditional Irish people who quietly maintain the old ways today understand very well that the "hidden teachings" of the tradition (a level of knowledge that Tibetans refer to as *terma* in their own tradition) dwell *within* this mandala, as well as in the land, which the Irish Spirit Wheel can be said to represent. Indeed, the whole island of Ireland *is* this wheel, represented by the later division of the island into four provinces — Connacht, Ulster, Leinster, and Munster — with a central or "middle" land, Midé, known today as Meath.

These are not mere philosophical concepts, or hollow New Age notions; they are the lifeblood of the primal Irish sacred view.

When working with the mystery traditions of the island of Ireland — what one keeper of sacred sites near Sligo refers to as the "island of initiation" — over time we will feel supported by the energies of the wheel beneath us. As we bring aspects of our spiritual journeys and life situations to the wheel, we will gain an increasing awareness of how these life-affirming energies truly yearn for us to succeed, to be liberated from suffering (including the suffering we exact on ourselves), to be happy, to be healed and whole. Rising up from the gallant turf of Ireland, and from the landscape of our own souls, the sacred wheel of prosperity, music, knowledge, battle, and sovereignty can lead us to a life beyond fear, filled with love and courage. In order to gain an even clearer sense of these principles, let us take a look at what I refer to as the *deeper energies of the wheel*.

THE DEEPER ENERGIES OF THE WHEEL

Devotees of the wheel know that the spiritual knowledge that dwells in the West of the mandala (the direction traditionally associated with the Celtic Otherworld) must be approached in a particular way — in earnest, with pure intent, without the narcissistic dramas of the ego that the modern world spawns. They understand that knowledge of the West is not just "head knowledge" but also "heart knowledge," as well as visionary knowledge gained from observing and opening oneself to levels of consciousness beyond ordinary reality.

The potent tempering energies of the North must be entered

into as a *conscious process* of soul refinement, as "spiritual warrior training." This direction is governed by energies requiring strength and humility; here we must hold healing, spiritual development, and authentic empowerment as our goals. If we do not, an encounter with the energies of the North can simply lead to unchecked aggression and cyclical violence — against others or ourselves, in the form of negative thoughts or soul-enslaving addictions.

Though some have summarily dismissed the associations of "battle" and "rough places" in the North as irrelevant notions left over from a bygone Celtic era characterized by swords and shields, the *inner* teachings of the North guide us into a different understanding of battle — a journey of learning about the shadow, about emotion, and about the battle that often develops between the ego and the soul (sometimes referred to as the higher and lower selves). Many people often experience the inner teachings of the North as a challenge, because these energies leave no stone unturned, including those aspects of ourselves we prefer not to look at.

The true spiritual prosperity that is the promise of the Eastern *airt* depends on our sense of gratitude for what we have, on our spirit of generosity and hospitality toward everyone — regardless of race, culture, or species — as well as on our coming into right understanding about the spirit of place, the nature of abundance, and the shadow side of consuming. The *inner* teachings of the East ask us to become good householders, in the Buddhist sense: tenders of space and the people who visit that space. Rather than always seeing how we can "get, get, get" or extract what we want from life, we begin to ask a new question: *How can I become the offering?*

In the South we have the Óran Mór, or the Great Song, one
of the old Gaelic names for God, the Divine. This is the music of
inspiration governing the life of the bard or poet who is in tune
with divine inspiration (Irish: *imbas*; Welsh: *awen*). Another way
to put it is to say that the great flow of life is symbolized by this
music; the vibrations of music that are felt and heard but not
seen represent the powerful invisible world behind the visible
world. It is the sacred world embedded within the profane world.
Some view the Great Song as the music of a world that stands
beside this one. In either case, then, the Great Song is a way of
thinking and experiencing a spiritual reality that binds the visible
and invisible worlds.

This "music behind the world" is the harmonious rhythm and
melody of being, known to us through our senses, through our creativity, through nature and dream, indeed, even through the wisdom and bubbling music of waterfalls. When we forget the music
of life, either within the world or ourselves, trouble soon follows.

In the Celtic way of seeing, the strength of an individual, of
a family, of a community, of a nation, and of the ecosystem can
be compromised when we ignore or neglect the sacred law and
order of these directions. When the harmony of right relationship, goodwill, and pure intent is lost, when the quest for wisdom,
peace, and balance is replaced by calloused greed, cancerous consumerism, violence, or unrefined energies, then the center of the
circle, characterized by an authentic spiritual sovereignty, can
become endangered.

Here *sovereignty*, in the primal Irish sense, refers to more
than just the sovereign boundaries of a nation. It is characterized
by an overarching sense of balance (and the daily pursuit of it),

protection of the land, and an underlying reverence for life. Ultimately, this life-bestowing, life-honoring power is the sacred energy that dwells at the heart of the Irish Spirit Wheel. Let us turn to a real-life example of how these energies can influence a life, and how we, too, can become forgetful of the sacred prin-ciples that help to maintain a sense of harmony.

Michael: An Angry Warrior Guarding a Tender Heart

At one time in his life Michael was utterly filled with rage. A former Israeli soldier who had moved to the United States to attend university, he had a fierce and persistent temper. More than one marriage had ended because of his temper; he had lost jobs over it; and, at one point, he was ordered by the court to take anger-management courses because of an incident occurring on the job.

I met Michael when I was still doing counseling. In my first moments with him I instantly sensed a lot of imbalance within the North of his wheel. He had seen a lot of violence, and he had perpetrated it, and he wore it all like armor around his shoulders, neck, and chest.

Because he had served successive tours of duty in Palestine, Michael's daily situation was governed by brute warriorship. From his story it was clear to me that every successive loss and failure in his life was brought about by his temper; ironically, these were times when Michael was trying to make changes in himself. The people around him had grown accustomed to his temper, so even when he made a great effort to change, people did not recognize these attempts. This made him angry, his temper would flare, and his inner battle would rage on. Michael's efforts to find some solidity and a sense of personal sovereignty always seemed to backfire. This was largely because his efforts were rooted in ego and in his ideas of how things should be (while he often disregarded the needs and wishes of others).

Michael was trying to restore the proper order of things in his soul, but at every turn he seemed habitually to slide back into "macho energy" rather than into the authentic strength of the awakened warrior or into the wisdom of the Universal Monarch, symbolized by the king or queen at the Center of the wheel. (We will explore this in further detail in the next chapter.)

In our work together, I set up a "wheel" on the floor, marking each of the directions with an object to symbolize the different attributes of the Irish Spirit Wheel. I encouraged Michael to step into the direction where he felt called. Predictably, he went with his intellect and stepped into the direction where he unconsciously felt most comfortable (a sign of his habitual armoring). He deduced, "My imbalance is in the area of battle and the warrior. I will step into the North."

While he stood in the North we discussed what it had been like for him to be a soldier. I asked what he had seen and done. With every question I asked, each time looking at how his response related to the North and battle, Michael began to get very angry. His face turned red, and his body became rigid. I encouraged him to keep going into the energy of the North. What was his anger trying to tell us? Repeatedly he defended his actions as an Isreal Defense Force soldier serving in Palestine.

As we tracked the true source of his rage, Michael suddenly found himself drawn to the South. This choice was inexplicable at first, and I thought he was simply avoiding the uncomfortable energy of his anger (and what really lay beneath it), but I've learned to surrender my "bright ideas" and to trust in the inherent intelligence of the process. As Michael stepped into the South, I reminded him of the energies dwelling there — music, inspiration, poetry, melody, sensuality, a connection to nature, waterfalls, the Óran Mór — none of the attributes one typically associates with warriors.

When Michael heard about the Óran Mór, the hardened soldier began to weep. For several moments he stood, grief rippling through his body. The "waterfall" had been set loose. As he spoke, Michael's whole demeanor changed from one of rage to one of deep tenderness.

"I, I . . . killed a child," he whimpered, covering his face with his hands. "It was an accident, but I feel so ashamed. When that happened, I stopped believing in God. What God allows such things to happen?"

Michael had opened himself to the flowing energy of the wheel and was guided directly to the insights he needed. We did a great deal more work together that I will not go into here, other than to say that it involved looking even more deeply into the psychological trauma of being a soldier. A recurring theme of our work, though, was the acknowledgment that in order for Michael to reclaim his personal sovereignty and the way of an awakened and enlightened warrior, he would need to restore his connection to that which he had turned his back on: God.

Let us now continue our journey into the deeper principles of the Irish Spirit Wheel as a way to remember and return to a spiritual way of seeing.

PART 2

THE IRISH SPIRIT WHEEL

REFLECTIONS AND MEDITATIONS

4

CENTER

Sovereignty — That Which Dwells
in the Middle of It All

The Lineage of Enlightened Warriorship

Disconnection from Sovereignty as Invitation

Sovereignty as the Divine Feminine

The center of any mandala grants the seeker access to a holistic perspective. The center encourages an integrative sensibility, in which we are deepened by the collective lessons of all the other directions. The poet David Whyte has a wonderful saying: "Anything or anyone that does not bring you alive is too small for you." In the Center of the Irish Spirit Wheel we are brought alive, we deepen our connection to our fullest selves, we are humble, secure, and ruled by grace rather than fear. Each of the sacred directions of the Irish Spirit Wheel demands that we step outside ourselves, and in the Center we are asked to connect with the magic and beauty of serving life.

CENTER

SOVEREIGNTY — THAT WHICH DWELLS IN THE MIDDLE OF IT ALL

*The enlightened kings and queens of the past, as well as the
ascetics meditating in caves, have all said that the secret of
creating stability is to put the welfare of others before our own.*

—— SAKYONG MIPHAM

In the primal Irish traditions, Sovereignty is a goddess. She holds
the center of the wheel, the living hub of energy that connects
all the directions, the *axis mundi* to which all paths ultimately
lead. In this context, sovereignty is the core, the heart of our life.
Every day we must all be able to answer these questions: Am I
in good standing with my destiny? Am I in good standing with
my life? Am I standing within my sovereignty?

In the ancient stories, the goddess of Sovereignty presents
herself in various forms and, in the end, bestows "rulership" on
those who are in right relationship with her — but not until they
have heeded certain requests. This is no less true of our lives:
our sovereignty and destiny depend on whether or not we have
listened to and heeded the requests of our souls.

In one ancient story, we encounter the goddess Sovereignty,
not only as a kingmaker, but also as a shape-shifter and a dis-
penser of sustenance:

One day, Niall Noigíallach (Niall of the Nine Hostages)
and his brothers went traveling. At a certain point in their

travels they became thirsty and began to look for water. Eventually they located a source of pure drinking water — an ancient well — but found the well guarded by a hideous hag. The hag demanded a kiss in exchange for water.

Two of Niall's brothers — Fergus and Ailill — were repulsed by the old woman and refused to grant her a kiss. They returned from the well empty-handed, and thirsty. Another of Niall's brothers — Fiachra — being somewhat sly, gave the crone a quick peck on the cheek, thinking that would suffice. It did not. She scowled at him and sent him away. Clearly, she had more in mind.

Niall, however, agreed to her demand, even going beyond it. While Niall's brothers, thirsty and cold, shivered by their fire, Niall was sated and warm, for after he kissed the hag, it is said that she revealed herself to him as a beautiful maiden and that the two laid together for the remainder of the night. In the morning, she unveiled her true identity to Niall: Flaithius, or Sovereignty. Not only did she give Niall water, but she also declared that he would have the kingship of Ireland, as would many generations in his line after him.

This ancient tale portrays one of the deep truths of primal Irish tradition: initiations — be they spiritual rituals, the making of kings, the inspiration of poets, or the shaping of warriors — often occur at the hands of the feminine, the Goddess, and often the *Cailleach*, a wizened crone figure, who can have a fierce and

challenging presence one moment and a sweet and tender coun-
tenance the next.

In ordinary reality, Sovereignty is represented in the Irish
landscape by a standing stone at the Hill of Tara. Covered in spi-
rals and other engravings, this upright monolith is called the *Lia
Fáil* and stands about four feet tall. It is also known as the Stone
of Dán, or the Stone of Destiny, *dán* being a word from Old
Irish (Gaelic) that has multiple meanings, each referring to a different expression of energy. The energy of *dán* expresses itself in
congruence with the *airts* of the Irish Spirit Wheel: *dán* as destiny (Center), *dán* as poem (South), *dán* as fate (West), *dán* as
boldness (North), and *dán* as gift (East).

The oral traditions tell us that this stone at Tara, at the Center of the Irish mandala, was one of four sacred objects brought
to Ireland by the ancient race known as the Tuatha Dé Danann.
It is told that the stone would sing or shriek when a man destined
to be king sat on it or leaned against it. In effect, the stone would
announce whether rulership was part of a person's destiny.

Adhering to an ancient pattern found in different parts of the
Celtic world, for thousands of years at this stone — the Center
point in the Irish Spirit Wheel — individuals accepted the mantle
of leadership, merged with the mandate of sacred energy of the
island, bonded with the goddess Sovereignty, and became married to the land — of which they were expected to be good stewards, caretakers, and protectors.

In many ways, it is the same with our lives; the powers that
bestowed our life on us fully expect us to be good stewards of it.
In our reflections and meditations on the Irish Spirit Wheel, it is

at the Center where we begin our explorations, and it will be the Center to which we will return.

The core association in the Center position on the Irish Spirit Wheel is sovereignty. Falling within this sphere at the Center are the additional associations of enlightened warriorship, dignity, mastery, destiny, and stability. Ultimately, the Center is about our life force and whether or not we are in good standing with its flow and wisdom.

The archetypal figure that sits at the Center of the Irish Spirit Wheel is the Divine King or Queen, both of whom are oriented to a life-affirming view symbolized by the life-giving Goddess. To use terminology from the Shambhala tradition, the presence or guiding energy at the sacred Center is the Universal Monarch.

Though most of us are not in a line to ascend to an actual throne, becoming a spiritual sovereign — in the primal Irish sense — resonates deeply with what Tibetan teacher Sakyong Mipham calls "ruling your world." This spiritual sovereignty is a cultivated state of mindfulness and energy that creates a royal bearing within us. Such a state gives us access to all the inherent wisdom energies that dwell in the four directions.

Having spiritual sovereignty doesn't mean that we are perfect; it doesn't mean that we don't struggle, that we don't have bad days, or that we don't experience conflict — far from it. Yet although we may become forgetful of the path we strive to walk, as the Shambhala teachings (the universal teachings of disciplined bravery) tell us, "The warrior's awareness is like an echo." Something always brings us back to Center.

While it does not mean we are perfect, it does, however,

mean that rather than settling for a life that is a high-tension drama factory, driven by habitual conditioning, unchecked impulses, avoidance and ego-anchored agendas or addictions, we aim to consciously conjure or invoke the Big Life of our soul: the enlightened energy of dignity, primacy, and destiny that is our divine birthright. In the case of Sarah — a creative young woman I encountered when I was still doing counseling — the Irish Spirit Wheel served as a reminder of her deep passion for creativity and the unlived life waiting for her just beneath the surface of her addictions.

Sarah: Smothering the Big Life of the Soul

Sarah, an attractive woman in her mid-thirties, introduced herself to me as a "very spiritual person" who had "trained in Buddhism" and "made her living as an artist." Though she presented a very positive image, I continued to sense something tumultuous beneath the surface, as if she were masking some great struggle.

In time, the truth of her situation began to reveal itself. After I asked her a few piercingly focused questions about what I intuited, her happy-go-lucky spiritual facade quickly began to crumble. Sarah became nervous. My questions seemed to get under her armor, to the heart of the matter. I attribute this not to anything I did, but rather to the power of "seeing" through the "eyes" of the Irish Spirit Wheel.

Sarah confided that she had taken up a habit of sniffing cocaine, and that addiction and impulsiveness were permeating her existence. She told me that she had begun to make some highly questionable financial decisions, for example, not paying bills so as to support her habit. She began to complain about her daily level of fatigue, as well as her lack of funds. I pointedly asked about the cost of the drugs, which she quickly became defensive about and began to qualify, saying, "they aren't drugs ...they are just my way to relax." Sarah said, "I don't do this a whole lot...just when I am tired, or feeling depressed about being broke."

I asked her how often she was tired and depressed about being broke. She grew quiet, and then responded, "I guess these days, most of the time."

After a while, I proposed an experiment. Because she identified herself as a "very spiritual person," she seemed intrigued. I invited her to visualize a circle, and I proceeded to describe the five points on the Irish Spirit Wheel, without going into depth about its origins. I simply focused on the particular attributes of each *airt*. I had her "face the East" in her visualization and then had her "walk" with me around the circle as I described it.

I encouraged her to move from one direction and its associations to another, taking time to step into each place in her mind's eye. Being an artist, she said she "liked the South" but "didn't like the North at all." She said the West "felt dreamy" and that she "couldn't really relate" to the East.

As I continued to describe some of the qualities beyond the core associations, I could discern a very subtle shift in her expression. The body never lies. She looked truly sad. I asked for clarification of what was happening for her. Sarah reported that she felt the energy "in front of her" (East) as the home she never had growing up, and she felt very frustrated about her lack of prosperity or means to manifest a home for herself that felt good.

At the same time, when she "tuned in" with the South of the Irish Spirit Wheel, she had a bittersweet feeling. For her, the South was not so much about music as it was about art, something she had gotten away from and that brought her great joy.

I then added, "All of us have a first love, something to which we dedicate our life energy. Some first loves can build our life up, and some of them can tear it down or prevent good things from happening for us. What's your first love?"

The process dropped into a very deep place and led to something of an epiphany. Sarah admitted that she hadn't done any art since taking up her cocaine habit. This disturbed her greatly. Sarah began to comprehend that to reclaim her personal sovereignty (Center), and her art (South), she needed to rid herself of these life-sapping addictions (North), find a new vision for her life (West), and truly explore what it would mean to extend hospitality to her own soul (East).

Within one year of exploring these topics using the guiding energies of the Irish Spirit Wheel to fuel and inspire her, Sarah became substance-free, financially more stable and secure, and an award-winning photographer with gallery openings in the United States and Europe.

And so turns the wheel....

When we are in right relationship with the energies at the Center of the wheel, we tenderly hold our life as a gift. Standing in the Center we can look out to the horizon, the East, the South, the West, and the North, and we can comprehend that each of these directions has lessons and different perspectives to offer us.

At times we may feel we have lost our path, or that it has lost us. Despite these feelings — even in the face of loss, disease, or our own impending death — a person manifesting the spiritual sovereignty of the Universal Monarch can embrace all aspects of his or her human experience as part of the path.

MEDITATION

Everything has been leading to this. There has never been a time when you have not been on destiny's path. All paths lead to the Center.

CENTER

THE LINEAGE OF ENLIGHTENED WARRIORSHIP

This wisdom does not belong to any one culture or religion,
nor does it come only from the West or the East. Rather,
it is a tradition of human warriorship that has existed
in many cultures at many times throughout history.

— CHÖGYAM TRUNGPA

We are always on the path. Even when we are in utter despair, we are still walking the path toward our spiritual sovereignty.

Even when we feel we have lost our connection to our deepest, wisest expression, we still have a dormant seed of spiritual sovereignty within us. If we work toward creating the proper conditions for growth (just as we would when sprouting plant seeds), the seed of our spiritual sovereignty will quicken to life. Certainly there are times when we feel very far from our sacred center, very far from any sense of connection to peace, harmony, or the proper order of things, as prescribed by our souls. At those times it can be helpful to remind ourselves that our journey on the wheel of our life is leading somewhere, that it *is* evolving, and that we *are* evolving right along with it.

A person working toward embodying the sacred destiny and spiritual sovereignty has a certain attitude about life. It is marked by a consciousness of spiritual warriorship or focused bravery that has been known to many people, in many traditions, throughout time. In the Celtic way of seeing, we welcome everything as a potential and auspicious teaching from the field of our life. When we walk the path of the Universal Monarch, therefore, we can find gratitude and sacred knowledge even in the midst of our struggles, even in a world that is topsy-turvy, a world that has seemingly lost connection to its spiritual sovereignty.

It is easy to think of ideas such as spiritual sovereignty, peace, and harmony as naive and idealistic. When we read the front page of the newspaper or listen to the latest broadcast of NPR news, sovereignty — in the deepest spiritual sense — seems hard to imagine, and even harder to come by. And it is nearly impossible to fathom that any society has ever managed to cultivate these qualities.

Yet many societies and communities have managed to embody spiritual sovereignty. The Tuatha Dé Danann of Ireland, the Kogi tribe of Central America, the Haudenosaunee (Six Nations Iroquois Confederacy), and numerous other indigenous people around the world have been exemplary expressions of the energies associated with the Center of the Irish Spirit Wheel. Like those who follow the Shambhala teachings, these various earth-honoring, spirit-aligned people have manifested enlightened warriorship in universally recognizable ways.

Likewise, when reviewing history we can take note of certain individuals who made their life journey one of profound self-cultivation and refinement and who — through their open hearts, focus, and discipline — have been able to manifest extraordinary lives imbued with an undeniable sense of peaceful warriorship and spiritual sovereignty. Gandhi, Eleanor Roosevelt, Morihei Ueshiba, Aung San Suu Kyi, Martin Luther King Jr., Rosa Parks, Thich Nhat Hanh, Thomas Merton, Peace Pilgrim, Julia Butterfly Hill: the list goes on.

Perhaps you know individuals who are embodiments of peaceful warriorship. Whether they are quiet presences in your life or world famous, it is truly empowering to hold such exemplars of spiritual sovereignty as your guides, as your spiritual ancestors, as supporters of your path who stand behind you in a long line of brave, open-hearted people.

Buddhist master Chögyam Trungpa described this collective of people — both known and unknown — as the "lineage of enlightened warriors," individuals who have appeared in every culture, manifesting brilliance, creativity, boldness, and peace. When we hold them as our guides, their bravery and their royal bearing set themselves up within us as well. We can invoke these guides; we can be nurtured by them. We step into the lineage with them and begin to speak with the voice of the lineage itself. We are the lineage.

Here is a meditation you can use, especially at times when you feel particularly challenged.

MEDITATION

I am not alone. I am accompanied. I stand within the lineage of enlightened warriors behind me, supporting me to manifest my most bold, creative, and enlightened self.

CENTER

Disconnection from Sovereignty as Invitation

We must be the change we wish to see in the world.

—— MOHANDAS GANDHI

What do you see when you look at the world? Many practitioners of Celtic spirituality who are familiar with these teachings see a world that has lost its spiritual sovereignty.

So many people struggle with addictions, abusing themselves with toxic food, drugs, harmful relationships, and poisoned thinking. They haven't found (or they have lost their connection to) a true vision for their life. The addictions take their toll energetically, emotionally, and often financially, thus depleting their life force and their finances; their day-to-day existence is often characterized by a lot of drama, conflict, tension, and stress. Rather than feeling a sense of gratitude — a quality that envelops and radiates outward from one who has embodied the energies of the Center (and the teachings of the Eastern *airt*) — those who have lost their sovereignty are often deeply bitter that life has not delivered the things they deeply long for.

A number of contemporary governments have become sidetracked from their authentic sovereignty. Some neglect the poor and the elderly, while others dismiss global warming while assaulting the environment. Some political leaders slash education and social programs, while simultaneously turning a blind eye to human rights violations and the desperate need for humanitarian efforts all around the planet. Still other leaders pass bills and tax laws that benefit the richest 1 percent of their country.

And, as you read this, Ireland — a land of people richly endowed with both a spiritual and a natural heritage — watches as their government turns a deaf ear to the traditional lore keepers of the island and marches forward with a plan to build a superhighway through the sacred Boyne River Valley, near the Hill of Tara, the location representing Ireland's sovereignty.

Elected officials using their positions to benefit themselves rather than the people; large corporations dumping toxic chemicals into rivers with no regard for wildlife or the people who may live downstream; military sonar shattering the peaceful songs (and hemorrhaging the brains) of whales in the sea; megastores buying products made in China, despite being conscious that such products finance the genocide of the Tibetan people; consumers buying millions of tons of chocolate per year, the vast majority of which (as of 2005) is produced through forced child labor on the Ivory Coast: each represents a world that has lost its spiritual sovereignty.

As we read the news and learn of these — and other — conditions, certain words begin to assert themselves in our consciousness: *Imbalance. Insanity. Illness.* In the face of high-velocity modern living, and our increasingly plasticized, disconnected, and anonymous lifestyles, many people begin to feel overwhelmed or despairing at their accumulated exposure to and knowledge of these imbalances.

In the Celtic way of seeing, however, the deep feelings that emerge as a response to these conditions are a call from the lineage, a call from the "spirits of the wheel," from God, or from the Goddess herself, to explore how we can effect change. When looking through the lens of the Irish Spirit Wheel, we see the imbalances in the world, in our lives, and in the lives of those around us as an invitation to embody and act on the deeper powers and energies of the sacred directions. We seek to invoke their influence, lessons, aid, and inspiration. We strive to align the center of our being with the Center of the wheel. We start the journey of the wheel within, committing to doing the work.

EXERCISE

Set aside a few minutes each day, perhaps ten minutes to start with, gradually expanding the time to thirty minutes a day. Contemplate this question: *What sacred life instructions does the wheel have for my life? How can I transform the things that prevent me from living according to the sacred instructions of my soul?*

CENTER

SOVEREIGNTY AS THE DIVINE FEMININE

See, we used to worship God as a mother.

— SINEAD O'CONNOR

Everywhere we hear a call to remember the divine feminine. From Riane Eisler's *The Chalice and the Blade* to the book and movie *The Da Vinci Code*, in which ancient Christian concepts such as *Sophia* (the feminine expression of divine wisdom) and figures such as Mary Magdalene are brought to life in intriguing ways. It seems as if the modern world is responding to a deep calling for a wisdom that is nurturing and intuitive rather than forceful, that is compassionate and heart-centered rather than intellectual.

In the Celtic perspective, the divine feminine is a wisdom-bestowing goddess. The great Irish war hero Cuchulain learns both fighting techniques and the inner wisdom of a warrior-in-balance from Scathach, a goddess on the Isle of Skye. A number of poet-seers in the Irish and Scottish traditions experienced and related to the goddess Brighid as the patron of poetry and fire. She acted as a muse for those poets who endured sensory deprivation, often seeking their quickening verses alone in the darkness of caves.

In the Western world we have largely lost a connection to the feminine as divine and as an orientation point for our lives. The divine feminine tends life, yet in a world where the orientation of this divine feminine is not allowed to exist, an imbalance is spawned. This imbalance enables governments to turn a blind eye to the destruction of the planet; it is the same imbalance that enables individuals to adopt a stoical, self-deprecating approach to their own lives. In truth, it is a psychological schism, a disconnection from accurately perceiving the nature of reality as it is. If we truly saw the nature of reality — such as how our decisions affecting the environment will affect many generations yet to come, for better or for worse — then we would take great care to alter our course in many ways.

The same can be said regarding our relationship to our bodies. If we do not genuinely perceive the connection between our bodies and the earth, both are imperiled. The environmental crisis is not a crisis of the environment; it is a human self-esteem problem. We don't truly value ourselves, our bodies, each other, all of life, and because our human bodies are extensions of the body of the earth, we take our low self-esteem, our self-hate, and create discord in the very thing that sustains us.

Sometimes we do need to draw on the intensity or bravery

of the warrior in the Northern part of the Irish Spirit Wheel to get things done in life, but if life becomes governed by that energy without the balance of gentleness, somewhere along the way the divine feminine is forgotten. To truly remember the preciousness of life, the warrior (the masculine qualities within both men and women) must surrender to the Goddess (the feminine energies within men, women, and the land). Hence the old Irish saying, "Never give a man a sword unless he knows how to dance." We aren't talking about a jig here. We are talking about the dance of integration.

MEDITATION

Life can be a blend of strength and gentleness. The Irish Spirit Wheel inspires us to bring our lives into balance. Are you aware of any imbalance within or around you?

5

EAST

Prosperity

Householding and the Energy of the Home

Hospitality to Others

Hospitality to Oneself

E ast is the place of abundance, prosperity, and householding.
The energies of the East teach us about extending good
energy, taking care of the body, and valuing our dwelling places.
We all spend most of our time in three places: at work, in our
homes, and in our beds. No one in their right mind would settle for
sleeping in a bed full of fleas or on a bed of nails, and yet all too
often we settle for workplaces and living spaces that are not truly
nurturing of our souls. The guiding energies of the East on the
Irish Spirit Wheel instruct us to care for self and other. Each of
the sacred directions of the Irish Spirit Wheel demand that we step
outside ourselves, and in the East we are asked to connect with the

importance of serving others while maintaining the healthy balance required to tend to our own health and well-being.

EAST

PROSPERITY

He who knows he has enough is rich.

— LAO-TZU

The core association of the Eastern *airt* in the Irish Spirit Wheel is prosperity. The other associations are hospitality, householding and householders, and gratitude. The archetypal figure that sits in the East is the Hearthkeeper, a sacred role in the Celtic traditions and a living symbol of hospitality, abundance, and good tidings.

When this governing principle of the Eastern *airt* was articulated in ancient Ireland, there were no stock portfolios, savings accounts, or rollover investment funds. People's relationship to the sustenance of their lives, to the passing of time, and to the reality of material goods was very different. Without a doubt, when contemplating prosperity, we can (and should) take into consideration our financial solvency and sustainability; however, this is not our focus here. Though we can apply a cultivated consciousness of prosperity to this area, we must first establish and kindle such a consciousness within.

As we open ourselves to the Eastern direction of the mandala, we can reap benefits at a deep level: our fundamental relationship to the "spirit of prosperity" as it relates to the living energies of the universe, especially as we experience them in the forms of love, food, our bodies, our homes, and the activity of acquiring things.

All too often we approach our relationship to prosperity from a fundamental perspective of scarcity. We don't believe there is enough to go around. We don't believe there will be enough for us. As a result, many of us grow lost in acquisition and consumption, driven by a deep unconscious belief that if we buy, buy, buy (or eat, eat, eat), we will somehow route our fear. Yet such an approach does not alter the beliefs themselves, and our beliefs shape our reality.

I have often thought that the origins of our fears about scarcity may be even more ancient than we realize. Could it be that somewhere deep within us, stitched to our ancestral DNA, we fear that the Great Mother is going to withhold her harvest? Outwardly we may have lives of relative comfort, and yet often we don't appreciate what we have because we are ruled by powerful unexamined sentiments within our psyches. Perhaps we have been raised by parents who operated, daily, from the fear-based assumption that what they had would be taken away because they had, in fact, suffered great losses. In some cases, our fears about scarcity may stem from the experiences of relatives and recent ancestors who lived through the Great Depression, famines, or various forced migrations.

The problem is that when we approach life from a perspective of scarcity and combine this with the infection of materialism, which tells us we must acquire more and more to be happy, we set ourselves up for failure and till the ground for potential addiction and depression. Our unbridled, unrefined consumerism becomes a self-fulfilling prophecy. Whether we try to sate it with artery-clogging food, soul-enslaving drugs, multiple sex partners, or gas-guzzling Hummers, such gluttony does not address the inner vacuum we often experience as citizens of the modern world.

To assuage our fears about scarcity we fill our homes and garages with objects that quickly prove incapable of meeting our most genuine need: a conscious relationship to the vital energies of life. Then, having depleted our resources in order to chase a fleeting sensation or perception of abundance, two things set in: the realization that we still feel empty of something for which we feel the deepest of longings and the awareness that we have manifested the very conditions of scarcity that we were hoping to avoid.

The antidote to this feedback loop of dysfunction is to cease our habitual tendency to think of both scarcity and prosperity as external phenomena, instead honestly taking stock of our internal state — including our basic relationship to our life force.

Until we courageously engage in that honest assessment, we will never truly know the sacred teachings of the Eastern *airt* of the Irish Spirit Wheel.

MEDITATION

The universe holds an abundance of energy. May we learn to manage this energy properly so that we may embody the spirit of prosperity, taking care of ourselves and others.

EAST

HOUSEHOLDING AND THE ENERGY OF THE HOME

You may live in a dirt hut with no floor and only one window,
but if you regard the space as sacred, if you care for it with your
heart and mind, then it will be a palace.

— CHÖGYAM TRUNGPA

One of the attributes associated with the Eastern position on the
Irish Spirit Wheel is the energy and practice of conscious householding.

Being a householder — in the Irish sense — is not as mun-
dane as simply owning a house. Much to the contrary, what I am
referring to here when I use the word *householder* is someone
who tends the spirit of her home, who focuses on making her
dwelling place an oasis of good energy, imbued with a feeling
that nurtures everyone who enters. As hearthkeepers, householders do not tend the energy of their home just for their own
sake, but also for the sake of visitors. In the Celtic way of seeing,
this care and tending are extensions of the energies of heaven.

Householders know that blocked or cluttered energy in the
home will eventually manifest as blocked energy in the psyche.
In many cultures, it is common knowledge that the soul of the
home and the souls of those living within that home are intertwined. We see this in the ancient Taoist practice of feng shui
in the Chinese culture, where meticulous attention is paid to
the alignment of objects, the design of structures, and the relationship of the front door of the home to certain directions.
Likewise, in the ancient aesthetic sensibilities of the Japanese,
great emphasis is placed on compact, uncluttered living, where

living spaces are governed by principles of minimalism and naturalness.

From the Celtic perspective, cleaning and organizing our homes is not considered a chore or a burden. When we "doctor our space," we attend to the shape and feel of our homes. Whether we are arranging objects in our homes to invite reflection or eliminating the clutter that can become a bottleneck of proper energy flow, this practice is a form of soul work. As Anthony Lawlor states in his wonderful book, *A Home for the Soul: A Guide for Dwelling with Spirit and Imagination*, "Cleaning is the act of discerning what will benefit our homes and removing what will not.... Cleaning allows us to discern those objects that enhance the flow of soul in a home from those that stifle that flow."[1]

We affect the atmosphere in our homes by our presence and the state of mind we bring into it, and vice versa: the energy in our homes has a direct impact on our state of mind. In turn, we take the energy of our dwelling place back out into the world. In this way, our homes become very powerful gateways of potential spiritual practice, transition points that — if worked with consciously — can transform us and inspire others. Attending to the energy in our homes does not mean we must have expensive art and top-of-the-line furniture. Excessive wealth and materialism do not constitute the kind of prosperity we find when we work with the energies of the Eastern *airt*. With very little money we can work with the energy of our homes, invoking a quality of elegance and harmony. Take some time to think of your home as more than just a place where you store your "stuff." Does your house truly feel like an oasis to you and to those who visit?

If your home is a place of stress and tension, or of clutter and blocked energy, dedicate some time to doctoring the space, invoking elegance, peace, and the proper order of things. If you find yourself instantly saying to yourself, "I'll get around to it later," set a date for a party or social gathering that you will host, with the intention of extending hospitality to others as a house-holder and hearthkeeper. Such events have a way of rallying our energies toward doctoring our homes.

MEDITATION

Our homes are an expression and an extension of our minds and hearts. Inner clutter and discord is expressed as clutter and discord in our homes. How we take care of our-selves is often how we take care of our home. As we work with the sacred energies of authentic spiritual prosperity, may we tend to our heart and to the hearth of our home.

EAST

HOSPITALITY TO OTHERS

A generous heart is never lonesome.

— JOHN O'DONOHUE

One way of perceiving and relating to the core energy of pros-perity in the Eastern part of the Irish Spirit Wheel is by extending energy to others — by being hospitable. If you have traveled to Ireland, then you have experienced firsthand this ancient code of Celtic hospitality.

Hospitality is a conscious approach of extending goodwill, of harnessing our own prosperity (whether in the form of monetary wealth or in the form of service, love, kindness, attention, tending, or food) and showering this abundance of positive life force on someone else. When someone bestows the prosperity of genuine hospitality on us, it leaves a sacred marking on our souls. It touches us, uplifts us, and helps us feel that we are not alone in the universe. Sometimes extending hospitality can be as simple as brewing a cup of tea and sharing several moments of silence together. I have a friend from County Mayo, Ireland. She is a nun and a healer, and despite her obvious connections to the Catholic Church, she is also deeply in tune with the primal Irish traditions that predate the Church. She once shared an idea with me that sums up the essence of Irish hospitality: "You've always got to be mindful of the stranger, the visitor, to show them kindness and hospitality. You never know if the stranger at your door is actually an angel or one of the good faeries."

Some people who work deeply in the Irish tradition extend this way of seeing beyond the domain of Irish society or even of the human world. They know that to truly work with the sacred energies of the Eastern *airt* one must adopt an ever-present practice of extending kindness and tending energy to the "sacred other" — whomever that sacred other might be. He or she might be a person of another race or another religion; indeed, that person may even be someone we originally perceived as a threat or an enemy. The sacred other might also be a creature or a patch of earth that has no one to protect it.

EXERCISE

See what kind of day you have when you allow yourself to see every person, every creature, every living thing with whom you come into contact as a "sacred other," a living thing worthy of respect, kindness, and hospitality. Who knows? You may even learn there are angels or good faeries in your midst.

EAST

HOSPITALITY TO ONESELF

True self-respect is not selfishness, but our duty to the soul and its soul-shrine: it includes caring for our body, mind, soul, and spirit, enabling us to relate to those who give us love and support, as well as those who challenge and stretch us.

— CAITLIN MATTHEWS

Ordinarily when we think of hospitality we immediately think of the kind we extend to someone else or that we receive from someone else. But another type of hospitality is that which we extend, or do not extend, to ourselves.

Many people have been raised in families in which they were conditioned to place others and others' needs before themselves, at all costs, a very unhealthy pattern. They may have been required to grow up very fast. Perhaps a family business, a chronically sick parent or sibling, or an entrenched addiction such as alcoholism defined every aspect of the family's identity.

With such dynamics some people lose the ability very early to tune in to their own needs, which become completely smothered by the situation. Now as adults, such individuals are hard-pressed to define their preferences, much less to truly take care of themselves. They have been programmed to think of taking care of themselves as being selfish. And they tend to have very deep-seated feelings — sometimes even on an unconscious level — that they didn't get certain needs met as children.

In an effort to seek a kind of psychic equilibrium, some people who were not taught the path of true self-care will desperately seek to fulfill the unmet needs of childhood in their adult relationships, or in other situations, which only serves to deepen their dissatisfaction or pain. They may seek the healthy intimacy they did not receive from a parent, for instance, in a string of unhealthy relationships or sexual encounters, desperately attempting to fill the void.

Some who were never emotionally nourished may try to find that nourishment through food addictions and overeating. Sadly, such people often become overweight, a condition that leads either to further rejection and/or to even more layers of self-hatred. Other people may develop a spending addiction so as to feel a sense of "richness" and "fullness" in their lives, resulting in a perpetual cycle of feeling empty, since objects and gadgets cannot truly bring happiness.

The wisdom of the Irish Spirit Wheel asks us to consider that if we extend to others when we are depleted or take care of others without taking care of us, we set ourselves up for illness, resentment, and pain.

MEDITATION

We cannot genuinely extend care, love, or hospitality to others if we also do not genuinely extend it to ourselves. If we do not truly learn the art of self-care, including the basic love of our own human journey, no one can really trust us when we say we care about them. Learn to relate to yourself as you would a visitor. How can you tend yourself with grace, elegance, dignity, and kindness?

6

SOUTH

Music

Óran Mór: The Great Song

Sweet-talkin' the Universe

The Music and Blessing of Waterfalls

S outh is the locus of inspiration, creativity, and the unbridled passion of the poet's heart. The South is where the human soul falls in love with the music of life. From the melodies and harmonious strains associated with literal music to the invisible "music" spinning within cells, molecules, and electrons, the powers of the South speak of the Great Music, the Great Song, at the heart of all Creation. Each of the sacred directions of the Irish Spirit Wheel demand that we travel deeper into ourselves, and in the South we are asked to connect with the vitality and power of the cosmos around us and within us.

SOUTH

ꝳUSIC

*From the gene pool of possibilities, an evolutionary mandala emits
the music of chance as the ecstatic, electric body emerges in an
awakened state of eternal becoming.*

— STEVE ROACH

The core association of South on the Irish Spirit Wheel is music.
However, as with the other parts of this mandala, the Southern
airt contains multiple layers, including the poetic life, inspiration, melody, and waterfalls, as well as advocacy, sensuality, and
a connection to the rhythms of nature.

Like the perspectives of many shamanic and mystical traditions around the world, the Irish and Celtic spiritual view of
music is quite expansive. The Celtic way of seeing holds music
as sacred, having potent capacities to carry us into greater connection to the spirit world, as well as healing and transformative
powers. In the Irish tradition we find ancient stories about music
consisting of "three strains" — laughter and joy, sadness and
keening, and healing sleep. Whether through listening to and experiencing the effect of these three ancient strains or feeling the
shaping powers of inspiration that bring forth expression from
deep within us, the music of the South stokes our emotional, passionate, and sensual connection to life.

In this sense music is not just a collection of musical notes
linked together like a string of pearls, or simply the melody made
by particular instruments working in unison. The energies of
the South also include an understanding of the "music behind the
world." This music behind the world can come through actual

music, our dreams, our time in nature, entheogenic (psychotropic) experiences, and our connections with other people.

The archetypal figure of the Southern *airt* is the Bard. In Celtic culture the bards have always been the gifted ones, multi-faceted characters who have sometimes been harpers, pipers, fiddlers, and *seannachai* (shawn'a'key), or "storytellers." Regardless of their instrument of choice, the bards are always poets, filled with an unmistakably lyrical way of seeing and being, lovers of the green world of nature.

We do not have to live like the Zen poets of Japan, the Sufi dervish poets of Persia, or the Celtic poets of Wales, Ireland, and Scotland to tap into the inspiration, sensuality, and creativity of a poetic life. Our poetic life, aligned with the pulsing music of existence, is waiting for us, right beneath our own feet. A poetic and musical life may even be a silent one, embodying what the great Irish seer, poet, and author W. B. Yeats sometimes called a "fierce life of quiet." The South on the Irish Spirit Wheel is not about committing words to paper or reciting stanzas. Instead, it speaks to a love affair, an ongoing dance with the turning days and nights of our life.

SOUTH

Óran Mór: The Great Song

Divine sound is the cause of all manifestation. The knower of the mystery of sound knows the mystery of the whole universe.

— HAZRAT INAYAT KHAN, SUFI MYSTIC

In many energy-sensitive cultures around the world (such as indigenous, earth-based, or Buddhist cultures that have a profound

awareness of subtle energy) we find as part of their cosmologies
a story about all life originating from an original sound and
about some strand of the original music — as frequency, vibration, and rhythm — being contained within all of life.

In the traditions of India, for instance, we find the concept of
Nada Brahma, which translates as "God is sound," or "the world
is made of sound." Similarly, I have heard Native American
medicine people refer to the origins of the earth and of our own
bodies as rhythmic emanations of an original heartbeat at the
center of the universe. When we open ourselves to the wisdom
energies of the South, we are opening to this "original music"
that flows through all things.

In the oral traditions of both Ireland and Scotland we find
people who have long known of this original music. Though it
has been manifested in different ways, a conscious knowing of
the ancient "music behind the world" has always been woven
into the daily awareness of the adherents of various Celtic traditions. For many practitioners of Celtic spirituality this primal
music is known as the Óran Mór. In the words of Stuart Harris-
Logan, a Gaelic healer, scholar, and author of *Singing with
Blackbirds*, "Out on the Isle of Barra, the people have long spoken of the Óran Mór as one of the old names of God. The Óran
Mór is the Great Song from which all things have arisen."[1]

My own first experience of the Óran Mór, which I relate in
my first book, *The Mist-Filled Path*, occurred one night in the
Kilmartin Valley in western Scotland. Sleeping within ancestral
barrows or on top of graves is an old Celtic custom associated
with communing with the ancestors and seeking insight, wisdom, and healing knowledge. That night I was guided to go out

into the night and to slide myself down into one of the open graves in the Kilmartin Valley, specifically one called *Ri Cruin*, the Round Grave of the King.

The cold night air was filled with a variety of eerie sounds and sights. Dogs barked in the hills surrounding the valley. Cowbells could be heard in nearby fields. Unknown visitors seemed to be kicking through the nearby grass. Glimmers of the aurora borealis could be seen off to the northwest on the horizon. A quiet moon arced across the sky. Clouds gathered off to the west, blocking any sight of the stars.

At a certain point, nestled down in the stone depression that formed the grave, I began to hum, partially to comfort myself and partially to stay warm. I shivered in the grave for a number of hours, meditating. Eventually, my humming began to ease my nerves and soothe my mind. I drifted off to that place between sleep and waking, feeling peaceful and calm. At one point I had a sensation of warmth; it felt as if a feminine presence had gathered close to me. Continuing to hum, I fell off to sleep. In an instant, with no awareness of how much time had passed, I awoke. My humming had been transformed to a deeper, more guttural form of throat singing (a form of chanting found in various shamanic cultures). I was throat singing involuntarily. Simultaneously, I became profoundly aware of a vast network of sounds that seemed to originate from a variety of places all at once — the stars, the sky, my own heart and the "sound chamber" of my chest, the stone and earth around me.

The sound permeated everything.

What I experienced put me in touch with something dynamic and vast, truly beyond my human faculties of speech to convey.

It was awe inspiring and humbling, and it left me with the unshakable sensation that life on Earth is not some sort of random anomaly of rock, water, and "accidental DNA," but, rather, a deeply purposeful pattern, an intentional blueprint of living systems bound together by vibration, beauty, energy... and sound.

I had felt the music of the universe *in* everything, including every one of my cells. It was, to use a different expression, an instance of connecting with the "music of the spheres," of God, the Tao, the Great Mother's lullaby: it was the Great Song.

All this may sound quite fantastical to our discursive minds, which all too often seek to analyze and categorize. However, conditioned intellect aside, your soul knows about the Óran Mór, for its tremulous vibration is within you, and your life a unique, uncoiling expression of it. What might it be like to wake tomorrow and agree, *fully*, to live out that expression?

EXERCISE

Allow yourself to become aware of the diverse sounds around you. Start with the simple sound of your own breathing at night, and in the morning as you drive to work. Maybe you have an almost involuntary impulse to sing in a hot shower. Perhaps you will become aware of the subtle nuances of sound that surround you every day — the rhythm of engines and elevators, the "song" of your washing machine on its spin cycle. Sometimes when I truly want to get back in touch with the Great

Song I listen to some of Steve Roach's music on my iPod. Tracks like "Return" from his CD *Dreamtime Return* or "Gone from Here" on his CD *Vine, Bark & Spore* put me back in touch with my initial experience of the Great Song. His sound-guided visual DVD called *Kairos* is also one of the most potent tools I know of for remembering the Great Song. In any case, whether you do it through music or through attuning to the "song of nature," if you need to feel realigned with life and the deeper magic of your life, you only have to go as far as the music.

SOUTH

SWEET-TALKIN' THE UNIVERSE

There are some people who will tell you that Celtic shamanism is about power. I say it is an ancient way of falling in love with the world around you, and within you.

— TOM COWAN

Each of the *airts* on the Irish Spirit Wheel is a living energy with which we can enter into relationship. In the South we encounter a profound energy that promotes devotion, awe, and a sense of falling in love with life.

This inspirational energy is so expansive, so permeating in its capacity to stir our hearts awake, that it is difficult to find words to express it. This is why the ancients referred to the

South simply as "music." Yet, for many people who work with the energies of the South, something else actually becomes activated within them: the power of poetry.

The mysterious spirit-man who transmitted the wisdom of the Irish Spirit Wheel to Fintan spoke of music in the South, but he also spoke of poetry, the poetic spirit being an important source of inspiration for the Celtic way of seeing. When we interact with the wisdom energies of the South and truly allow ourselves to be shaped by its inspiration, we find ourselves seeing the world through the eyes of a poet. It is not about being an Oxford-trained specialist in iambic pentameter. The wisdom and inspirational power of the South says, "If you can observe life, if you feel it in every trembling leaf, if you can give voice to that, you are a poet." The seventh-century Irish text known as the *Cauldron of Poesy* suggests that poetry is an inner light that everyone has within them but that only shines forth in those who pay attention to and learn to follow its power.

The bardic tradition, especially as seen in the rich storehouse of Celtic nature poetry, is an unbroken cord of devotion. Through making a profound connection with the spirit of place, Celtic poets have always expressed their love for the land, becoming a voice for the land. This is why "advocacy" is included in the ancient associations to the South on the Irish Spirit Wheel. Ancient Celtic nature poems — often unsigned by the author — praised a certain tree, bird, mountain, or river. Contemporary poets such as Sorley MacLean (1911–1996) carry on this spirit by injecting the reader with an emotional sense of place, loss, and tradition. The stunning use of verse, in MacLean's poem "Hallaig" is one example. The practice of giving voice to both the beauties and injustices of life is inseparable from the Celtic soul.

One of my dear friends, the Celtic mystic and author Tom Cowan, is deeply moved by and infused with this sense of Celtic soul. He has revived a very old Irish practice that is an expression of this type of poetic devotion. It is called *geancannach*, which translates roughly as "love talk." It is both an ancient form of poetry called a "praise poem" and a very personal kind of daily practice, one rooted in tradition and in our love of life.

Celtic "love talking" is essentially a meditation practice that hails from the deeply inspired states of consciousness of the wandering bards. With all the nature adoration of a Mary Oliver poem and all the passion of a verse by Jelalludin Rumi, Celtic love talking isn't about writing "good poetry"; it is about living it in each moment. In Celtic love talking we *become* the poem. *Geancannach* is about your relationship to nature, to the life around you. It is about speaking that devotion and adoration directly to the forest, the mountain, the waterfall, a human lover or friend, or the Great Shaper of Life. The question is: Do you love any place or person so much that you will open your heart, eyes, and mouth and say so?

In some of Tom's retreats and deep soul work with people, he initially shares a bit of the style, rhyme, and meter of some of the old love-talking or praise poems, and then he requests that people go out into nature and *become* the practice. Like so many forms of poetry from indigenous traditions, the praise poems often follow a kind of set formula that facilitates greater memory as well as a trancelike rhythm of vocal meditation. One of the many formulas that Tom suggests is: *Beautiful...beautiful too*. For example, as you step out of your door and encounter the day, you might see a number of sights or feel a variety of sensations that make an impression on you. You might say: *"Beautiful is the purple sky at sunrise; beautiful, too, is the soft morning breeze. Beautiful the sound of swaying oak branches in the wind; beautiful, too, the sound of the chirping wren."*

In the practice, the person typically keeps this cycle of verse going for quite a while, walking through the forest, taking in the fullness of life and reciting one's praise poem as an offering to the spirit of life, to the universe.

Despite its seeming simplicity, I find the love-talking practice to be one of the most powerful remedies for depression. As I have sometimes said, the *antidote to depression is devotion.* Tom's reenlivened practice of Celtic love talking is a potent way of entering the consciousness of devotion and of losing ourselves again in the divine embrace of the living earth.

MEDITATION

Often the great tragedy of our lives is that we don't take time to notice. Another tragedy is that often we don't say what we mean, and then it becomes too late. What would it be like to spend an entire day in Celtic love-talking consciousness? Though it might be challenging, try it anyway. Approach a variety of people and natural phenomena and, holding those people or living things in mind and heart, say, at least to yourself, as a meditation: "Beautiful...beautiful, too...."

SOUTH

THE MUSIC AND BLESSING OF WATERFALLS

*The diviner was wrapped in the hot skin of a newly slaughtered ox
and laid at full length in the recess behind a waterfall. Clad in the
"cloak of knowledge," his mind in a ferment, his ears deafened by
the roar of the water, his garbled answer to the question put to him
was considered to come from the spirit who haunted the falls.*

— ELIZABETH SUTHERLAND

When Fintan learned of the many other wisdom energies of the
Irish Spirit Wheel, he heard something curious uttered about
the South, the realm of music. He found that, in addition to
music, the knowledge and wisdom of the South also concerned
inspiration, advocacy, and...waterfalls.

Waterfalls?

At first glance this may seem a bit odd, but when we allow
ourselves to soak in the real "juice" of the South it makes perfect
sense. For the South is also about sensuality, connection to nature,
and beginning our transition in consciousness from the material
reality of life (householding in the East) to the knowledge of the
spirits in the West (the direction associated with the Otherworld
in Celtic tradition).

The South, then, becomes a kind of transition point, a gateway from the human world to the spirit world, specifically
through the world of nature. In the druidic path of the Celtic
tradition it is precisely through the sensual world of the body
and nature that we find God, the Goddess, the divine. It is in this
realm that we become intimate with the ancient music.

In the Scottish Highland tradition, seers often sought water-falls as locations for moving from the physical world to the spirit world. Some have conjectured that it is the lulling sound or even the roar of the water that entrances us and enables us to shift our consciousness. Others, such as Lakota author A. G. Ross, have gone so far as to say that it is the negative ions — which are in abundance at and around waterfalls — that become a catalyst for visions and inspiration. Whether these visions are due to the pleasing sound or the negative ions is really not our concern. The fact of the matter is the act of sitting quietly at a waterfall can create a profound shift in consciousness — which is worked with not only in the Celtic tradition but also in the indigenous nature religion of Japanese Shintoism.

Some years ago the spiritual energy of a waterfall had a poignant and tender effect on a friend and me. We were hiking in the hills of the Catskills and we came upon a bubbling brook and a line of stones over which a small wall of water fell. It was one of those places that seemed to invoke the spirit of peace, and for the two of us, who always seem to be looking for stopping places at which to sit and meditate, it provided a nice respite from our walking.

After a while we both stood up, and it seemed only natural to bestow a blessing on one another. My friend bent down to the river and offered some lavender, cupped his hands, drizzled the water over my head, and said a druidic prayer over me. I did the same for him, and we left the place in silence.

Some may read the above account and respond, "So what?" They are obviously still standing outside the Irish Spirit Wheel.

For me, as I journey through my busy life, I can tap into my mythic memory, reconnect with the sound of that waterfall, link up with that special moment, and just as if the water had been freshly drizzled over my head, I can feel the living energy of that druidic blessing and prayer. When I do, I stand just a little bit taller, my heart becomes fuller, and I feel, at least for a while, that I have come back into alignment with the Great Song of Life.

MEDITATION

We must give ourselves permission to connect with the flowing music of nature.

WEST

Knowledge

Longing and the Knowledge Within

Counsel

Vision

A thirst can form in our souls that drives us to embark on a journey. This thirst is the thirst for sacred knowledge — what the ancient mystery schools throughout time and across cultures have thought of as *gnosis*, as *dharma*, as *medicine*. In the Celtic traditions the West is associated with the spirits, the Otherworld, and the ancestors. Ancestors, in this sense, can be biological ancestors or "spiritual ancestors" — individuals whom we are related to through spiritual affinity though not necessarily through heredity. Each of the sacred directions of the Irish Spirit Wheel demands that we step outside ourselves, and in the West we are asked to connect with the wisdom and knowledge of the invisible world.

WEST

KNOWLEDGE

There are many different kinds of knowledge.
The way of the heart and spirit can guide us
in a more trustworthy way than the intellect alone.

—— BUCK GHOSTHORSE, LAKOTA SIOUX MEDICINE MAN

The core association of the Western position on the Irish Spirit Wheel is knowledge. Within this sphere are the additional connotations of longing for the Otherworld, seeking vision, learning, and the importance of story in conveying depth of experience.

In the Celtic way of seeing, knowledge is not limited solely to "head knowledge." There are visionary ways of knowing. There are deep forms of knowing that we might call "heart knowledge" or "body knowledge." Anyone who has heard a fully impassioned poet or singer has been in the presence of heart knowledge. Anyone who has seen a fully embodied dancer or a well-trained practitioner of Aikido has witnessed body knowledge.

Similarly, within the primal Celtic traditions and various shamanic traditions worldwide, there are other ways of knowing involving levels of experience that are not relegated to the intellect, or head knowledge, alone. Psychic knowing, emotional intelligence, and intuition, as well as the kind of precognitive and retrocognitive insight that typifies the life of the Celtic seer are also attributes of the knowledge of the West.

The archetypal figure that sits in the West of the Irish Spirit Wheel is the Seer. A seer is any individual who seeks to acquire sacred knowledge, whose heart is filled with longing for it, and whose path is a living expression of this sacred knowledge. In the Celtic world these qualities have manifested themselves in various figures through time, such as the hermit, the monk, the wandering poet, as well as druids-as-counselors and druids-as-shamans. Druids were considered the learned men and women of the Celtic tribes, people who specialized in different kinds of knowledge, from healing and vision seeking to offering counsel.

We live in a different era than did the druids, monks, and wandering poets of old. Indeed, almost nothing of modern life would be recognizable to them. Unlike those living in the ancient rural communities throughout Wales, Ireland, Scotland, the Isle of Man, Cornwall, and England, we are disconnected from one another and from the earth on which we depend. Not to over-romanticize their existence, but it is clear that many of the seekers-of-knowledge in the ancient Celtic world were profoundly oriented to the natural world and to a living wisdom and inspiration that sustained them daily.

Most of us cannot go back to living in land-based compounds, or even to having lifestyles governed by a much slower rhythm. And yet we do not have to run off to a forest hut, cave, or ancient monastery to return our awareness to the kind of ancient seeing that the druids and traveling poets possessed. It is a matter of taking the time in our busy lives to consciously open ourselves to levels of knowledge and experience that stand outside the intellect, of inviting the passion of the heart, the wisdom of the body, and the deep insight of the seer to come to the forefront.

WEST

Longing and the Knowledge Within

*If you have life within you, you have access
to all the mysteries of the universe.*

— MORIHEI UESHIBA

One aspect of human experience openly acknowledged by the Celtic way of seeing is the energy of longing. From the archetypal yearning for God (the desire to merge with the divine) to the classic Celtic motif of hungering for the Otherworld (a spiritual realm perceived by Celtic practitioners, often characterized by wisdom, knowledge, and a pristine sense of belonging), longing is one of the potent yet not always obvious qualities of the West. While some traditions view longing as an impediment to spiritual development, in the Celtic perspective longing allows us to become truly intimate with our deep humanity. In this light, longing becomes a trustworthy guide, an energy that leads us to what we need, if we are truly willing to pay attention.

Longing often sets up a dwelling place in the human soul. For the artist, musician, or poet, it can inspire some of the most compelling works of art. For the lover, longing for the other can sometimes become a very powerful (and at times painful) process of soul discovery. For the mystic, the longing for knowledge of and union with the sacred has led to using the language of desire, as do the Sufis, who speak of yearning for the Beloved (God). This same longing for vision and sacred knowledge drives the spiritual activity of the Western *airt*.

The longing of the West on the Irish Spirit Wheel becomes the quest for knowledge, the passion for learning, the desire for divine experience, and a deep sense of yearning for a vision to guide our life, what the Lakota tradition refers to as *hanbleceya*, or "crying for a vision." When we work with the energies of the West, it is almost as if we cannot rest, for the yearning to know and to feel connected to the wisdom that holds the worlds together becomes a singular quest.

One of the deeper teachings of the mystery traditions is that the longing for sacred knowledge and the sacred knowledge itself are intimately woven together. What you long to know seeks to be known. What you yearn to manifest has its own longing to be created and brought into form. What we long for wants just as much to be discovered, found, or expressed as we do to discover, find, and express it.

The sacred knowledge we desire is already embedded within us; we merely have to access it by putting ourselves into proper relationship with that knowledge, learning to trust the ancient language of the human search.

REFLECTION QUESTIONS

- What do you long for?

- How will you know it when you find it? What will it feel like?

- What do you long to know?

- What knowledge is trying to express itself through your longing?

WEST

COUnSEL

A person without a soul-friend is like a body without a head.

— OLD IRISH SAYING

We all lose our vision. At such times, we must seek counsel. From the perspective of the indigenous traditions, it is only the crazy person who does not seek help when conditions call for it. One of the secondary associations of the West on the Irish Spirit Wheel is counsel; the ancient and central role of Counselor was played by the druids of the Celtic world.

To seek counsel is, in essence, to seek the living wisdom and vision of someone we trust. We trust the wisdom they have cultivated as they walk the path of life, or, in this case, as they walk around the Irish Spirit Wheel.

When we hit a "rough place," such as those spoken of in the North, it is often our ego (or pride, also found in the North) that prevents us from having the humility to seek counsel. When we work with the Irish Spirit Wheel, we work out of our systems those egoic aspects that cloud our better judgment, that prevent us from seeking the resources that our wiser self knows would benefit us.

One of the great spiritual and emotional resources that has been part of the Irish tradition for a very long time is the *anam-chara* (soul-friend). The *anam-chara* is an ancient expression of seeking counseling in the Irish tradition. Originally of druidic origin, and later adopted and built on by the pre-Roman Celtic Christians, the way of the *anam-chara* is a process by which we form a deep bond with someone we can bear our soul to and who will listen deeply. Formally or informally, the *anam-chara* listens deeply to us and assists us in kindling our own inherent wisdom and self-knowledge.

As you travel the Irish Spirit Wheel, bringing your life issues to the wheel's different stopping places, you may find that your inner work is too overwhelming for you to process alone. In such instances you are encouraged to visit the West — the direction of learning and knowledge — and then to seek out the counsel of an *anam-chara*.

MEDITATION

It is a sign of strength to seek the counsel of someone we trust. Although she cannot walk the path for us, and she cannot solve our problems for us, an *anam-chara*, or soul-friend, can offer a safe space and encourage our deeper knowing to spring forth.

WEST

Vision

Where there is no vision, the people perish.

— PROVERBS 29:18

The Celtic way of seeing, and the Celtic spiritual traditions in general, are visionary. By *visionary* I mean that they bridge the inner and outer worlds — the "outerscape" of the natural world (and the various sources of energy, power, and wisdom that Celtic spirituality has long acknowledged there) and the inner landscape of the practitioner.

It can be difficult to discuss such things as the inner land-scape, because these ideas (and experiences) are quite foreign to modern sensibilities; we've been "educated" away from such deeper ways of knowing. After a visit to the South on the Irish Spirit Wheel, however, we find ourselves more in tune with our senses and sensuality, ready to seek the teachings of the West. We begin to have a greater comprehension of and fluency with the inner terrain of the soul. And it is precisely through the senses that we find the gateway to the otherworldly knowledge of the West.

Fellow poet and druidic practitioner Jason Kirkey states, "Soul and nature, the inner and outer landscape, are one; they are the wildness of the world and the wildness of the self. To alienate ourselves from one is to alienate ourselves from both."[1] The beauty of this sentiment lies in its ability to gently tune us in to the process of vision seeking. It encourages us to step into the natural world, the Garden we were never truly banished from, and to then consult the wisdom of the inner landscape, thus bridging both worlds.

It is within this state of consciousness that we can attune more closely and fully to the destiny of our soul, to track and even foretell what fate we may be living out. It is also within this state that we can ask the following questions.

REFLECTION QUESTIONS

- What kind of life do I want?

- What is my vision for the future?

- How can I live in more congruence with the "wild wisdom" within me?

- Am I denying the truth of or failing to truly live out my vision?

8

ΠORTH

Battle

Enlightened Warriorship and the Shadow

Addressing Addictions

The Magic of Conflict and Rough Places

Πorth is the place of tempering, challenge, testing, refinement, discipline, and facing the shadow. It is where we shed our fear, address addictions, and move from psychological and emotional enslavement to authentic freedom and power. The North is where we are stretched beyond the smaller, conditioned definitions we may have of ourselves. This direction presents us with life experiences that often feel like the proverbial black-belt tests. To help us to become strong and emboldened, the North often tests us so we may cultivate these qualities — all the while learning the difference between brute warriorship and sacred warriorship. Each of the sacred directions of the Irish Spirit

Wheel demands that we travel deeper into ourselves, and in the North we are asked to connect with the humility of the true warrior within, who is simultaneously strong and tender.

NORTH

Battle

Victory over oneself is the primary goal of our training.

— MORIHEI UESHIBA

The core association in the Northern position on the Irish Spirit Wheel is battle. Within this sphere of energy are also tempering, pride (ego), boldness, and rough places.

The archetypal figure sitting in the North of the Irish Spirit Wheel is the Warrior, who can have either an actualized and enlightened expression that leads to peace, discipline, and personal refinement or an imbalanced expression that can lead to violence, unconscious conflict, and even bloodshed.

On a personal level, when working with the energies of the North on the Irish Spirit Wheel, we *all* become *warriors-in-training*. If we truly open ourselves to the energies of the North (and sometimes our soul opens us to these energies without consulting us first!), we find that our life suddenly becomes a testing ground, part of a tempering process in which we are required to face off with our own worst enemy — the entrapments of the addicted ego.

Battle has long been associated with Ireland. Indeed, the ancient history of Ireland includes what we refer to as the "five invasions," and the more recent record (the 1600s on) involves other invasions as well, the karmic trajectory of which is still being lived out today in the literal North of Ulster.

One set of battles that forms part of the *inner* teachings of the North involves two groups of beings found in the ancient record, namely the Tuatha Dé Danann and the Fomorians. Sometimes known as the Shining Ones and the People of Peace, the Tuatha Dé Danann are associated with harmony, peace, and maintaining the proper order of things. The Fomorians, on the other hand, are associated with chaos, destruction, and upheaval. From the ancient Irish record we learn that these two groups engaged in two battles, known as the First and Second Battle of Moytura.

Different people in the Irish mystical traditions interpret these groups in different ways. Some see them as symbolic of the elemental forces of earth, constantly battling it out, with the abundant "greening powers" of life always seeking to flourish and propagate life, and the tumultuous and chaotic energies of nature — such as wild storms — attempting to wreak destruction.

Another way of perceiving them, however, is as forces linked to our own energy that can teach us about ourselves. In the traditional Irish view, each of the characteristics that we associate with these energies is needed to ensure the balance and proper order of things. We need the dark and the light. We need the heavy and the buoyant. We need the creative powers of life and — as uncomfortable as such times might be — we also need those times of challenge that test and temper us. It is only through such times and challenge that we learn how to harness our own potential as a source of strength and transmuting power.

NORTH

ENLIGHTENED WARRIORSHIP AND THE SHADOW

For the sake of mental stability and even psychological health,
the unconscious and the conscious must be integrated
and thus move on parallel lines. If they are split apart
or dissociated, psychological disturbance follows.

— C. G. JUNG

We are living in a time characterized by a heightened degree of projection. Citizens are projecting onto leaders. Leaders are projecting onto each other. Nations and members of various religions are projecting onto nations and members of other religions.

C. G. Jung and others have described projection as a process of placing outward onto others all the unconscious, disavowed, unacknowledged, and disembodied features of the psyche — what is sometimes referred to as "shadow material." The ego believes that by projecting this intrapsychic material, it will avoid having to work with or integrate it, avoid having its self-aggrandizing and pleasure-seeking agenda complicated.

The irony, however, is that it is precisely through projection that our psyches attempt to make us conscious of our shadow material, if we have not been working with it consciously as enlightened warriors. Jung warned that those aspects of the shadow that we do not make conscious will eventually be lived out as our fate. He also noted that becoming enlightened is not about imagining beings of light but rather about making the contents of the shadow conscious. We can make our shadow material conscious by truly attuning to whatever presents itself

to us in meditation, in dreams, as well as in our everyday interactions with people.

When we practice meditation it is quite common for shadow
material to make sudden appearances. Likewise, the shadow is a
frequent visitor to our dreams and to our conscious dream work,
constantly trying to educate and initiate us into the depths of the
psyche. Finally, in daily life if you find yourself suddenly having
a large emotional reaction without knowing why, you can bet the
shadow is stirring the energy. Learning to pay attention, to
track, and even to record the energies of the shadow (by journaling and dream journaling) is a very powerful practice.

Put another way, we may project the energy of our disavowed aspects outward, but this energy always comes home to
roost. Politicians, both liberal and conservative, whose choices
are driven by disavowed shadow material, for instance, may
manage to live above the law for a time, but no one is above the
laws of the psyche, and ignored shadow elements always attempt
to get our attention and can even be played out in the public
arena.

We all project. In the workplace we project stuff onto our
boss, our supervisors, and our co-workers, and bosses and supervisors project onto employees. This dynamic is nearly universal,
but it can also become destructive, especially in companies that
spawn a lot of volatility and competition or that do not have
processes in place for helping everyone stay conscious of the
shadow. We project in our friendships when we unconsciously
compare ourselves to our peers or even to couples to whom we
have become close. We may covet their accomplishments or pos-
sessions; alternatively we may also project our own problems

onto friends having similar problems in the form of judgment about their experience.

Projection also plays a large role in love relationships, from the early stages of romantic love — a very highly charged arena of projection — to the power struggles and conflicts that many go through when they let the petty ego rule instead of the heart.

We also project shadow material when we perceive individuals of other races, nations, sexual orientations, or religions as the enemy — the root of many battles. This phenomenon has always been stitched into the fabric of humanity. There has never been a time when we have not had to deal with the fallout of collective projection. If we are ever to evolve a culture of peace on this planet, we must become conscious of the potential harm of unconscious collective projection, one of the most significant pieces of shadow work we will ever have to master.

This level of projection is so potent because although it may express itself in the thoughts, words, and actions of an individual, its ultimate source is derived from a taproot that has been sent down into the deeper strata of the collective unconscious. When individuals begin to congregate around a shared process of projection, influenced by charged collective shadow material, it can lead to what we recognize as racism, hate crimes, and even wars.

This phenomenon is responsible for tensions between Christians and Jews, Catholics and Protestants, Hindus and Muslims, Christians and Muslims, whites and blacks, Republicans and Democrats, Labor Party members and Tories, prochoice and antiabortion activists, Serbs and Croatians, Irish and Brits, and the list goes on and on, in every culture around the world.

Reclaiming our projections is one of the most powerful ways to circumvent the imbalanced and unhealthy power of brute warriorship. By having the courage and heart to reclaim them, we can align with the energies of our birthright — dignity and authentic bravery — as opposed to brute strength guided by fear. This is the path of the peaceful warrior of the heart.

ᓕᓕᓕ

MEDITATION

By reclaiming our projections we can neutralize their energy. Are you projecting anything onto others right now? When you consciously reclaim your projections and cease to see the world through those filters, how does your perspective change?

ᓕᓕᓕ

NORTH

Addressing Addictions

Enemies such as craving and hatred are without arms and legs.
They are neither courageous nor wise.
How is it that they have enslaved me?

— SHANTIDEVA, EIGHTH-CENTURY BUDDHIST SCHOLAR

The wisdom energies of the North on the Irish Spirit Wheel are unique in their capacity to create change in your life. The North is the direction of tempering, refinement, and spiritual testing. For an enlightened warrior who is developing mastery in his life, including a sense of dynamic awareness about his life energy, the North is the place to cultivate an understanding of how certain things may have become what Robert Spenser, author of *The Craft of the Warrior*, refers to as "power leaks."

We could compare the energies of the North on the Irish Spirit Wheel to the swordlike qualities of the *vajra* spoken of in Tibetan Buddhism. *Vajra* translates as "adamantine" and is symbolized by a thunderbolt or a diamond. This image is a symbol of penetrating awareness, the kind that can cut through anything that is an obstacle to our spiritual development.

The wisdom energies of the North continually ask us to assess how we may be opening ourselves to influences that encumber us or even drain us of the life energy we need for walking the wheel. The North is where many people do the very necessary work of expelling addictions from their lives.

Addictions come in all shapes and sizes. Besides the obvious life-crippling reality of drug addiction, addictive activities are often more neutral. Many, such as shopping, eating, having sex, working, exercising, Internet surfing, "blogging," and so on seem less overtly harmful than abusing drugs or drinking to excess. However, because we may unconsciously be trying to extract something (often the fulfillment of some unmet need) from these activities that cannot be found within them, we start to mismanage impulses, which leads to obsession.

Anything that continues to entrench us in the pattern of addictive response — a person, a habit, a job, a substance (including food) — takes us away from the path of enlightened warrior-ship, mastery, and a life of authentic balance and sustainable contentment.

The metaphor of "doing battle" with an addiction can be very helpful for people who want to restore the proper order of things in their lives, but just as important is the need to gently embrace and befriend that part of them that may be driven by an addiction. The part of us that becomes obsessive also possesses wisdom and intelligence. Its longing is true; it is merely off track in where and how it chooses to meet that longing.

The wisdom energies of the North ask us to cease relating to the world in such an enslaved and impulsive way, to eliminate habits and patterns (including patterns of thinking) that keep us weak and small. When the seed of enlightened warriorship has firmly taken root, we see there is actually no need for battle at all — just cultivation.

NORTH

Tʜᴇ Mᴀɢɪᴄ ᴏꜰ Cᴏɴꜰʟɪᴄᴛ ᴀɴᴅ Rᴏᴜɢʜ Pʟᴀᴄᴇꜱ

Conflict is a fact of life.

— LAO-TZU

Most people fear conflict and confrontation. Maybe you are saying, "Of course. That's natural." But though many people will agree that these things are to be feared, that does not make the fear natural. Our collective agreement to remain driven by fear and to avoid conflict is not our divine birthright. Rather, our birthright is to embrace conflict for what it is: a profound gift, an opportunity to work together toward mastery, transmutation, and transformation. This is one of the deeper and more potent teachings of the Northern part of the Irish Spirit Wheel: *conflict is not bad*.

This ancient sensibility — that conflict is simply a powerful learning process containing heavy or dense energy — can be seen in the work of a variety of master energy-workers, from Arnold Mindell's *The Leader as Martial Artist* and Thomas Crum's Aikido-inspired *The Magic of Conflict* to Marshall Rosenberg's *Nonviolent Communication* and Deidre Combs's *The Way of Conflict*.[1]

These master energy-mediators deeply understand the wisdom of the North. Rather than having us avoid conflict because it requires energy, a state of vulnerability, and a fully attentive heart willing to transcend the petty ego, they enjoin us to call on our authentic boldness. They encourage us to enter *into* the energy of conflict with a willingness to investigate it in order for it to actually transform.

Doing so takes immense bravery and heroism; in Irish the word for warrior and hero are the same — *gaiscíoch* — and in Tibetan the word for warrior, *pawo*, simply means "one who is brave."

Although we in the modern world typically think of a warrior or hero as someone who rains down destruction and kills the enemy, the spirit-filled teachings of the mystery traditions and enlightened warrior paths show us that the true warrior, the true hero, is one who is willing to step into the center of chaos, to dance with it, to bring about harmony rather than destruction. Rather than feeding chaos with more violence, the true hero transforms it through being attentive and by mediating its energy.

One of the dearest practices in my life that has taught me the most about the *true* warrior spirit has been the Japanese martial art of Aikido. Unlike other martial arts, which are often rooted in an ethos of confrontation and destruction, Aikido has a purely defensive orientation, with the aim of neutralizing the energy of an attack in a nonviolent yet highly effective way. Though it ultimately hails from the ancient warrior traditions of Japan known as Bushido (the ways of the samurai), Aikido is guided by an underlying philosophy: the Way of Aiki. The Way of Aiki transcends the martial art itself and touches on everything, from dispute mediation and daily interactions with people, to how one walks across a room or sips a cup of tea. Its true meaning is the "way of manifesting the energy of harmony."

When working with the Northern part of the Irish Spirit Wheel, we may find that at a certain point in our development and learning, something very similar to the Way of Aiki comes to our aid. As we stumble into the rough places of our life, we can reframe the experience from "something is being done to me" to "I have received an invitation to become aware of my center, to blend with difficulty rather than running from it."

Whether the rough places manifest externally in the form of conflict or internally as personal struggles, the consciousness of the enlightened warrior can help us smooth out the rough edges, to see the irritation of conflict as the very energy needed to create the pearl of wisdom and possibility.

MEDITATION

Think about Morihei Ueshiba's words in the *The Art of Peace*:

The Way of a Warrior
Cannot be encompassed
By words or in letters:
Grasp the essence
And move on toward realization![2]

COΠCLUSIOΠ

Back to Center

*An intellectual interpretation of a symbol is by no means identical
to experiencing the energy embodied by that symbol.*

—— R. J. STEWART

Because there is a real difference between a mere description of the wheel and an experience of its actual influences (or the "energy embodied by its symbol," as Scottish seer R. J. Stewart reminds us), in this conclusion I suggest other practical ways of applying this ancient Irish mandala to your daily spiritual practice.

The symbol of the Irish Spirit Wheel, with its *axis mundi*

and its four points constituting the cardinal directions, can be viewed as merely an archetype or even as just a quaint artifact of ancient Irish consciousness. The true power of the wheel, however, cannot be conveyed by symbols or by brief descriptions; it cannot be grasped by the intellect alone. This book is merely a key. The door you can unlock with it is the domain of actual experience.

As practitioners we must graft the wisdom energies of the wheel onto our own body/minds and souls, approaching these repositories of guidance with an attitude of surrender, genuine openness, and receptivity to what may come through as an insight, emotion, or lesson. To approach an inherently holistic system, such as this Irish mandala, using the intellect only would be folly, the equivalent of getting lost on the "paraphernalia path" of spiritual materialism — collecting spiritual systems and models, gurus and teachers, or ceremonial items, thinking that such things in and of themselves hold the capacity to create the transformation within that we so desire.

To help you truly ground the wisdom energies of the Irish Spirit Wheel in your life, below I offer a few rituals for working with the wheel. Although these may seem rather simple at first glance, do not underestimate the potential impact of these kinds of gestures on the deeper strata of the subconscious. This is the true power of ritual.

Ritual is not about being seen; it is not about casting spells, earning merit, or placating a wrathful deity. It is a form of communication. Ritual speaks directly to a very ancient part of us.

In a sense it is the oldest form of transformational psychology, in that it creates change on the level of the soul. If the word *ritual* trips you up, or if *ceremony* sounds too stuffy and formal, simply think of the following suggestions as contemplative exercises.

The Irish Spirit Wheel Journal

The first thing you might experiment with as you begin working with the energies of the Irish Spirit Wheel is creating a journal in which you will record entries for the full turning of a year. Writing in a journal is one of the most tangible ways in which a spiritual practitioner can bridge the inner and outer worlds, second only to dream work (which often calls for writing in a journal as well).

Divide the journal into the five sections: Center, East, South, West, and North. These sections will be dedicated to the core themes and subthemes of the wheel, and as you work with the energies of the wheel, you are invited to record your thoughts, experiences, and insights within the relevant sections.

As you journey through the directions of the wheel, throughout the turning days and nights of the upcoming year, you can set aside specific times to review your journal and to take stock of the developments and learning that have taken place along a certain theme. For example, are you aware of differences in your experiences related to the spirit of prosperity from season to season? What did you "do battle with" in the fall, and what did you learn? And so on.

The Irish Spirit Wheel
as Problem-solving Tool

An added dimension of using the Irish Spirit Wheel (and the journal if you so choose) is exploring the wheel as a proactive problem-solving tool. This can be a very clear method for getting at the heart of a situation and for opening yourself to ways of bringing about the proper order of things.

However, as with all problem-solving methods, the person seeking understanding and resolution must be willing to embrace the truth that presents itself to her through the energies of the wheel and her own heart-centered intuition (another way of saying the Celtic way of seeing). The Irish Spirit Wheel, like any good counselor, isn't going to tell you what you're hoping to hear. If you work with its energies in an honest and forthright manner, however, it will guide you to clarity. Below is a simple five-step process for bringing some of the deeper questions of your life to the Irish Spirit Wheel for the sake of gaining deeper clarity:

1. Carry your problem or situation to the CENTER of the wheel. How does the issue relate to your sovereignty, destiny, or sense of mastery? Does the situation, person, or issue promote or diminish your sense of spiritual sovereignty? Remember the words of the poet David Whyte: "Anything or anyone that does not bring you alive is too small for you."

2. Carry your problem or situation to the EAST. With the inspiration of an energy-sensitive householder, have you done what you can do to optimize your

energy around the issue? Does your body relate to the issue; have you taken care of the "house" of your body? In what way can you extend hospitality to yourself around the issue? Are you sabotaging the prosperity in your life in some way? What can you do to sculpt a more sustainable way of being in relation to the issue? Hint: You already know.

3. Carry the issue or problem to the SOUTH. How have you adhered to or forgotten your own rhythm (the music of your soul) in relation to the problem or issue? What do the wisdom energies of the SOUTH suggest you need to do to restore yourself to your proper rhythm? Is part of the issue related to a fundamental lack of inspiration? Are you feeling disconnected from something, very far from the kind of harmony found in music? Suggestion: Spend time in nature and surround yourself with music that uplifts rather than depresses you. The energies of life augment whatever energies we surround ourselves with.

4. Carry your issue to the WEST. What are you longing for? Does the issue relate to some deeper knowledge that you need? Perhaps you are already "in the know" but you need the boldness of the NORTH to act on this knowledge. Contemplation: If you were told that you had three weeks or three months to live, what would you do differently?

5. Carry your issue or problem to the NORTH. Are you "doing battle" with something? Is it with someone

else, a situation, or a part of yourself? Does some part of you need to experience some tempering or refinement for the issue to be resolved? Are you aware of any habitual ways of thinking that consistently limit you? Do you have any "power leaks" that need to be addressed?

We Go Where We Need to Go

As you work with the Irish Spirit Wheel you will soon see that it is not just a nice arrangement of concepts or ideas: it is a living process that can lead us into an encounter with important issues that need to be resolved.

Probably the most helpful way of viewing the wheel, and the energy of each of the directions, is to see that each area invites initiation into deeper work. This spiritual or contemplative work can open us up to levels of life inquiry and life experience we have never before known. As we step through the gateways of each *airt*, we find that the spiritual energy of the wheel, and of particular directions, asks certain things of us.

From sacrificing habits or ways of thinking that keep us from truly living our destiny and sovereignty to assessing how our choices may block the prosperity that tries to flow into our life; from enveloping us in conditions that slow us down enough to examine the state of our heart and soul to catapulting us forward into experiences that call on us to live from a place of heart courage and boldness, the Irish Spirit Wheel — when we truly approach it as enlightened warriors — can become a path of mind training and soul tempering.

In effect, there is no way to authentically engage with the energies of the Irish Spirit Wheel without grappling with some of our often-unacknowledged issues and cultivating a sense of clarity, empowerment, and awareness. As we walk the wheel, it takes us exactly where we need to go. We may think that we are investigating the theme of a particular direction, but before we know it we find ourselves ushered into an encounter with the wisdom energies of a completely different part of the wheel and its life instructions. Sometimes we think we're headed toward the East, and instead we find ourselves standing in the North.

Wisdom and an almost relentless power are embedded in the energies of the Irish Spirit Wheel. They place us in the stream of energy we most need to bring about balance and refinement. When we truly embody these energies, we become a force aligned with life, a force that can restore the proper order of things.

ACKNOWLEDGMENTS

First and foremost I would like to thank my editor, Georgia Hughes of New World Library, for putting up with me again; and thanks go to Mimi Kusch and Kristen Cashman for tenderly midwifing the book into its final shape.

Additionally, I would like to thank my friend Darion Gracen for being a fellow dreamer and "horse thief," and for serving as my Jedi master at times. I stand in deep awe of your path, your journey, and your ability to teach us spiritual insight, but even more important, how to be fully human.

Many thanks must go to Tom Cowan; your unyielding and peace-kindling presence is such an inspiration to many. Your ever-renewing ability to stoke the Celtic love-talker in each of us is an unforgettable gift.

There is not room enough for me to thank the many individuals who have been a support to me, so I must express my gratitude in this fashion: thank you to the many women who have taught me about the different faces of the Goddess, and thank you to those refined, disciplined, and cultivated men and women who have taught me the authenticity that comes from walking the path of the spiritual warrior.

ПOTES

Book epigraph: Gabrielle Uhlein, *Meditations with Hildegard of Bingen* (Santa Fe: Bear & Co., 1983), 21.

FOREWORD

1. John Keats, in a letter to George and Georgiana Keats, April 21, 1819, in *John Keats: The Complete Poems* (London: Penguin, 1973; reprint, 1988), 549.

INTRODUCTION

1. Elizabeth Sutherland, *Ravens & Black Rain: The Story of Highland Second Sight* (London: Corgi Books, 1985), 26–27.

CHAPTER I.
MYTHIC MEMORY AND REMEMBERING
THE FUTURE

Epigraph: Caitlín Matthews, *The Celtic Spirit: Daily Meditations for the Turning Year* (San Francisco: HarperSanFrancisco, 1999), February 8 entry.

CHAPTER 3.
SACRED DIRECTIONS, LIFE DIRECTIONS

Epigraph: Morihei Ueshiba, *The Art of Peace*, trans. and ed. John Stevens (Boston: Shambhala Publications, 2002), 46.

1. In the Tibetan traditions there is a concept called *terma* that can mean "hidden teachings" or "recovered knowledge." The Shambhala teachings are considered to be a *terma*. These teachings are a concentrated body of lore that the late meditation master and author Chögyam Trungpa achieved access to and articulated in contemporary language. The ancient civilization of Shambhala is spoken of as an enlightened society that is either hidden within the Himalayas, or now exists in some other realm. The Shambhala tradition itself is the foundation for a secular contemplative path that seeks to initiate people into a spirituality of disciplined bravery, what Trungpa referred to as *enlightened warriorship*. Today, the Shambhala teachings are shared through a variety of programs at urban meditation centers and rural retreat centers. For more information about Shambhala International, visit: www.shambhala.org.

CHAPTER 4.
CENTER

Epigraph, page 52: Sakyong Mipham, *Ruling Your World: Ancient Strategies for Modern Life* (New York: Morgan Road Books, 2005), 192.

Epigraph, page 59: Chögyam Trungpa, *Shambhala: The Sacred Path of the Warrior* (Boston: Shambhala Publications, 1984), 5.

Epigraph, page 62: Well-known saying of Indian ascetic and nationalist leader Mohandas Gandhi (1869–1948).

Epigraph, page 65: Sinéad O'Connor, lyrics from "Famine," *Universal Mother*, compact disc, Capitol, 1994.

CHAPTER 5.
EAST

Epigraph, page 70: Lao-tzu, *Tao Te Ching*, trans. Gia-Fu Feng and Jane English (New York: Random House, 1972), 33.

Epigraph, page 73: Chögyam Trungpa, *Shambhala: The Sacred Path of the Warrior* (Boston: Shambhala Publications, 1984), 118.

1. Anthony Lawlor, *A Home for the Soul: A Guide for Dwelling with Spirit and Imagination* (New York: Potter, 1997), 39.

Epigraph, page 75: John O'Donohue, *Eternal Echoes: Celtic Reflections on Our Yearning to Belong* (New York: Harper Perennial, 2000), 308.

Epigraph, page 77: Caitlín Matthews, *Singing the Soul Back Home* (London: Connections Publishing, 2002), 237.

CHAPTER 6.
SOUTH

Epigraph, page 82: Steve Roach, liner notes from *Body Electric*, compact disc, Projekt Records, 1999.

Epigraph, page 83: Hazrat Inayat Khan, *The Music of Life* (Santa Fe: Omega Press, 1983), 43.

1. Stuart Harris-Logan, personal communication, January 2004; *Singing with Blackbirds: The Survival of Primal Celtic Shamanism in Later Folk-Traditions* (Ayrshire, Eng.: Grey House in the Woods, 2006).

Epigraph, page 87: Tom Cowan, personal communication, June 2003.

Epigraph, page 91: Elizabeth Sutherland, *Ravens & Black Rain: The Story of Highland Second Sight* (London: Corgi Books, 1985), 46.

CHAPTER 7.
WEST

Epigraph, page 96: Buck Ghosthorse, spoken during an Inipi sweat lodge ceremony, 1988.

Epigraph, page 98: Morihei Ueshiba, *The Art of Peace*, trans. and ed. John Stevens (Boston: Shambhala Publications, 2002), 11.

1. Jason Kirkey, "A Song from a Silver Branch: The Healing Power of Music," available at www.betweenthemists.org/silver_branch.htm.

CHAPTER 8.
NORTH

Epigraph, page 106: Morihei Ueshiba, *Warrior of the Light: A Manual* (Boston: Shambhala Publications, 2002), 165.

Epigraph, page 108: C. G. Jung quoted in Meredith Sabini (ed.), *The Earth Has a Soul* (Berkeley, CA: North Atlantic Books, 2002), 205.

Epigraph, page 111: Shantideva, quoted in Danielle and Olivier Follmi, *Offerings: Buddhist Wisdom for Every Day* (New York: Stewart, Tabori & Chang, 2003), June 14 entry.

Epigraph, page 113: Lao-tzu, *Tao Te Ching*, trans. John Bright-Fey (Sweetwater, OK: Cliff Road Books, 2004), 130.

1. Arnold Mindell, *The Leader as Martial Artist: Techniques and Strategies for Revealing Conflict and Creating Community* (Portland, OR: Lao Tse Press, 2000); Thomas Crum, *The Magic of Conflict: Turning a Life of Work into a Work of Art* (New York: Simon and Schuster, 1987); Marshall Rosenberg, *Nonviolent Communication: A Language of Life* (Encinitas, CA: PuddleDancer Press, 2003); and Deidre Combs, *The Way of Conflict: Elemental Wisdom for Resolving Disputes and Transcending Differences* (Novato, CA: New World Library, 2004.)

2. Morihei Ueshiba, *The Art of Peace*, trans. and ed. John Stevens (Boston: Shambhala Publications, 2002), 84.

CONCLUSION:
BACK TO CENTER

Epigraph: R. J. Stewart, *The UnderWorld Initiation: A Journey Towards Psychic Transformation* (Lake Toxaway, NC: Mercury Publishing, 1988), 36.

INDEX

Brighid (goddess), 66
bruadaraiche (dream-seer), 7
Buddhism, 11, 43, 83–84
　　vajra (swordlike qualities), 112

C

Cailleach (crone figure), 53–54
Cauldron of Poesy, 88
Celtic cross, 5
Celtic spirit, 17–18
Celtic storytelling tradition, 10, 18, 36
　　the Bard (*seannachai*) and, 83
　　mouth-to-ear transmission, 3
Celtic way of seeing, 3–4, 6–10, 40
　　calling from the "spirit of the
　　　　wheel" and, 64
　　everything as a teaching from
　　　　the field of life, 60, 114
　　as heart-centered intuition, 120
　　householding and, 73
　　Irish Four Directions and, 44
　　music as sacred, 82
　　myth and, 16
　　visionary ways of knowing and,
　　　　96–97, 101–2
Center (sovereignty), 34, 35, 39, 44–
　　45, 51–67
　　balance and, 44–45, 64, 67
　　dán and, 54
　　disconnection from, as invita-
　　　　tion, 62–64
　　example of Sarah, smothering of
　　　　Big Life, 56–58
　　Goddess dwelling in, 40, 46, 54,
　　　　65–67
　　Lia Fáil (Stone of Dan) as sym-
　　　　bol of, 54
　　meditations on, 59, 62, 67
　　people exemplifying, 61
　　personal sovereignty and, 47,
　　　　54–55

　　as sacred energy, 45
　　self-care and, 66
　　societies exemplifying, 61
　　spiritual sovereignty and, 59–62
　　story of "Niall of the Nine
　　　　Hostages" and the crone, 52–
　　　　53
Chalice and the Blade, The (Eisler), 65
Chartres Cathedral, 5
Combs, Deidre, 114
community, 41, 61
Conaing Bececlach, 31
conflict and confrontation, 113–15
Connacht, 41
Cowan, Tom, 87, 89
　　Beautiful...beautiful too for-
　　　　mula, 89–90
Craft of the Warrior, The (Spenser), 112
Crum, Thomas, 114
Cuchulain, 65–66

D

dán, 54
Dananns (Tuatha Dé Danann), 2, 31,
　　54, 61, 107
Darkwood, 31
Da Vinci Code, The (Brown), 65
"deep time," 16
divine inspiration (Irish: *imbas*; Welsh
　　awen), 44
dreaming
　　dream journal, 109, 119
　　Dreamtime, 40
　　lucid, wakeful, 8
　　"music behind the world" and, 83
　　seers and, 8, 9
　　shadow self and, 109
　　shamanic journey in, 40
Dreamtime Return (Roach), 87
Druids, 8, 97

I

ABOUT THE AUTHOR

F rank MacEowen is a writer whose journey has been influenced by primal Irish spirituality, cross-cultural indigenous
wisdom, and Buddhist mindfulness training. An alumnus of Naropa
University's graduate program in psychology, MacEowen continues to explore Zen practice, poetry, and the artistic process.
He divides his time between the American South and Ireland.
Visit his website, www.solasdana.org.